From Rabbit Ears to the Rabbit Hole

From Rabbit Ears to the Rabbit Hole

A Life with Television

Kathleen Collins

University Press of Mississippi / Jackson

The University Press of Mississippi is the scholarly publishing agency of the Mississippi Institutions of Higher Learning: Alcorn State University, Delta State University, Jackson State University, Mississippi State University, Mississippi University for Women, Mississippi Valley State University, University of Mississippi, and University of Southern Mississippi.

www.upress.state.ms.us

The University Press of Mississippi is a member of the Association of University Presses.

Some names and identifying details have been changed to protect the privacy of individuals.

Manufactured in the United States of America

First printing 2021
∞

Library of Congress Cataloging-in-Publication Data available
Hardback ISBN 978-1-4968-3229-0
Epub single ISBN 978-19-4968-3231-3
Epub institutional ISBN 978-1-4968-3232-0
PDF single ISBN 978-1-4968-3233-7
PDF institutional ISBN 978-1-4968-3234-4

British Library Cataloging-in-Publication Data available

Contents

The space between the television screen and whoever happens to be receiving it. I consider it very holy ground. A lot happens there.

Fred Rogers

Even knowing you are manipulated, you are still as helpless as the male butterfly drawn to painted cardboard.

Annie Dillard

Acknowledgments

Thank you to the board and staff (and benevolent peer reviewers) of the University Press of Mississippi who saw fit to include this project in their esteemed collection. Katie Keene and Lisa McMurtray were the initial shepherds; then Shane Gong, Lisa Williams, Jennifer Mixon, and their teammates skillfully and seamlessly carried on with production during a global pandemic.

I am grateful for the people in my life who allowed, encouraged, and accompanied me in my television watching, especially my parents, Judy and Jim; Grandma Deedle; Professor Ellen Willis; and my husband, Gerard. A very special afterschool-special thank-you goes to Amy Tucker for stepping up to be my first reader and for her spectacular memory as well as actual archives of relics from our shared past. And a vigorous nod of appreciation for all the razor-sharp TV critics, pop culture writers and podcasters for unwittingly bolstering my endeavor because they take it seriously, too.

From Rabbit Ears to the Rabbit Hole

Introduction: TV Matters

It's the dead center of a pleasant summer weekday in New York City at the Paley Center for Media—which I peevishly wish were still called the Museum of TV & Radio—and all the computers in the viewing library are occupied. Every few minutes I look away from my screen and, in the dim light, scan the faces of my headphoned comrades, who, like me, were probably chided as kids to "go outside!" on a sunny day. I'd like to tiptoe around to spy on everyone's screen, to see what's making them smile or stare open-mouthed or elbow-nudge their friend or laugh way too audibly. The only screen at which I can sneak a peek is that of the poker-faced guy next to me who is watching the performance of an eighties hair band. What's on my screen, you wonder? I'll tell you later.

There are other places to go for plentiful and free air conditioning, but something brought these souls here—to watch TV. They could have picked from thousands of programs from the library's long-tailed collection, a spot check of the entire history of TV, but they opted for that thing they're watching now. Like choosing one's last meal, it's specific, subjective, and revealing. It is the thing you love above all other things. It betrays a slice of the pie of your whole self. This is just one of the many pieces of evidence supporting my thesis: TV matters.

Like every person who's ever written about their childhood, I, too, have warm fuzzy memories of my local library. And while it fits nicely into the narrative of my eventually becoming a librarian, that's not my truest story. I read a lot as a kid—much more than I do now—but it's TV that tethers me to the core of my young self. The idea of me in front of a TV screen might lend itself to images less aesthetic and wistful than those of a little girl sprawled on the floor of a public library absorbed in the pages of a picture book twice the size of her head, but the truth is rarely idyllic.

This is the third book I have written about television. The first chronicled the history of TV cooking shows. After it was published, a colleague asked me what I was working on next. "The TV career of psychologist Dr. Joyce Brothers," I told her. "Wow, you're really changing tracks!" she replied. I was puzzled, because even if she didn't think in Venn diagrams, she had just heard me say the word "TV" twice in the span of twenty seconds and should have been able to discern a through line. But I suppose what she heard was "food" and "not food." I get it. Food is sexy. And as of about 1998, everyone seems to love talking about it all the time all over the place. So if it's in a couplet with another topic, it will beat the pants off that other topic hands down. Food is the sun around which all other topics revolve. Some people referred to me as a food writer after that first book. I disavowed the categorization out of respect to the many wonderful food writers in existence, and also, I am not a food writer, nor was it a book about food. Even more unreasonably and pointlessly, people began asking me for restaurant and recipe recommendations. If I wrote a history book about the Civil War, would I be a logical resource for musket-cleaning techniques? The second book, to my continued dismay, was often erroneously referred to as a biography. It was not one. Both were fundamentally books about TV. But apparently TV as a headliner is hard for some people to get their heads around.

Just to go on a bit more about food—see? it's compelling!—despite the currency of food as a subject in the general population, in the world of academia the idea of my book elicited a pleasant chuckle, meaning that when I told fellow faculty members what I was working on, their reaction was one of poorly veiled condescension toward what they likely saw as a silly topic but one they would back-pedalingly argue was a breath of fresh air rustling down their murky halls. Upon introducing myself in a meeting, the college provost said, "Oh, the one who wrote the cookbook!" "Well, no, but yes," I conveyed without bothering to explain that I was that one, but it was not. With regular people, when you tell them you're writing about TV cooking shows, they immediately launch into their own Food Network consumption habits, and at the time I was writing the book (and still is the case as I write this one), the panoply of programs on offer were all of the competition variety. I admitted to an acquaintance that I didn't really like those shows and didn't watch them much. She was stunned and asked why on earth I would write about them if I didn't like them. I should have deployed my Civil War–musket rejoinder. But her reaction is also an indicator of the low status of popular culture study, as if it can be observed from a fan's perspective only, not an analytical one. Obviously, I strongly believe both perspectives are not only possible but necessary. I don't want to kill the joy and pleasure of TV, but if I were to be a committed advocate for anything in this world, it would be for acknowledging how important TV is to our lives, like it or not, and therefore it should not be treated like a scatological event or a balloon animal.

When I was shopping around for a publisher for the book about cooking shows, one rep told me that people who watch TV don't read books. Obviously, my first and rageful thought was, "*I* watch TV, and *I* read books." He also said, "You want to make sure your book doesn't end up in the TV section in the bookstore. It's the kiss of death." Well, sure, because in most bookstores, if there even *is* a TV section, it's a puny misfit collection of books about shows. *The Simpsons* and *Buffy* fans might find something to feast on there—even though the area generally looks neglected and ragged, as if it were the designated place to drop off books that browsers decide not to buy or where employees haphazardly stash things they mean to shelve later—and read about the plots they've seen a hundred times, but other people (e.g., me) are bereft (and rageful). You might find books about the medium in a sociology section, but these are also scant and tend to be so rife with academic jargon that they are unreadable by most intelligent humans. TV is frequently slipped into the film and cultural studies sections. And so on. Rarely is the word printed on a section label of its own. But with about five bookstores left, it doesn't really matter anyway.

The problem with TV and bookstores—and maybe this negates the claim that it's a problem—is that TV is everywhere, in everything. So it's not wholly possible to pin it to a section. TV's seeming Achilles' heel, then, might actually be better viewed as its inherent strength. TV is a great companion to other topics, the way bacon is to any other food. Almost any subject matter has some relationship to TV. Put another way: TV is in everything and everything is in TV. If you find that a bit hyperbolic, then try this: TV is a lens through which to view any subject in modern life, a way to talk about everything. You'll find it, often disguised as mass media, in book indices in almost any history book about the twentieth century. That should not come as a surprise, given that TV *content* reflects and affects human existence in all its glory and defeat, and the *medium* itself broadcasts that content all over the place. As critic John Leonard has said, "Whatever the social problem, whatever the novelty in the culture, whatever the crisis or extremity of the culture, it's going to show up in one form or another on television." I know there are other topics that fall into this category, too. Food, for instance. But food has its own section, fetishistically subcategorized. This ambiguous "problem" is another piece of evidence supporting my thesis.

Libraries, thanks to rigorous and meticulous cataloging (especially with the user-friendly, mania-inducing cross referencing available now in online catalogs), are better than retail outlets at ferreting out where TV lives. But I was anxious when my first book, the one with the word "cooking" in the title, was being published. I desperately did not want it to be categorized as a food book, both for the aforementioned not-a-food-book reasons and the additional fact that I felt magnanimously responsible for adding to the scholarship of television, to help beef up the PN1992 (or 791 in Dewey Decimal vernacular) call number section. Putting my obsessive worrying into action, I contacted the Library of Congress to find out about the fate of my book and consequently my career and the future of television studies. Fortunately, for me and for humanity, it had been branded PN1992. And no disrespect to my beloved avocational field of psychology, but I also had fingers crossed that book number two, the one about the TV psychologist, would end up in PN1992. (It did.)

No mere tagging system, however, can bestow TV with a cosmic nod of approval, much less cultural value or meaning. TV was born with a tarnished spoon in its pie hole, and FCC chair Newton Minow's 1961 "vast wasteland" screed was a genie that was impossible to force back into its bottle. It's only roughly in the second decade of the twenty-first century that TV has managed to assume a somewhat sophisticated aura and properly rid itself—on the whole, let's leave reality TV out of it for now—of its trashy reputation, enough that anyone who harrumphs about its shallow content and worthless existence is rightfully written off as a fusty, out-of-touch troglodyte.

A sign of TV's ascendance appeared in a 2015 *Vulture* article wherein the author, Daniel Engber, praised television *content* but lamented the impoverished state of *talk* about it. Upon reading the title, "Your TV Small-Talk Is Ruining Dinner Parties," my hackles went straight into fight mode. But it turned out that I agreed with its auteur-provocateur on some points. We can't always talk about TV in a satisfying, intelligent way, as we can about movies. But it's a problem of logistics, that is, the conversation-killing "No, I haven't seen that" or "I've only seen the first season, stop talking!" It devolves too easily, Engber argues, into "Yes, oh my God, SO GOOD" and "a lame rehashing of the plot," leaving little room for dissent or intelligent discourse. And the divisive cultural bubbles, for example, *Downton Abbey* vs. *Duck Dynasty*, are putting up intimacy walls. If this small talk happens to you, I say, you're just attending the wrong dinner parties. For too long scholars were postulating that TV watching is incidental, something you do half-assedly while also doing something else, and that the visual immersion of watching movies makes it a more engaging and therefore more legitimate experience. That's drivel. Kids (and most adults) are not distracted when watching TV, whether it's a nineteen-inch Panasonic three inches from the face, a 110-inch wall mount a few more feet away, or an iPad. So, believe me, your formative experience of TV was legitimate and engaging.

But, yes, I crave deep TV talk, and it is hard to find. I find it with my husband, but Engber describes this relationship as one of those solipsistic bubbles: "This couple-talk only recapitulates the bigger problem, though. It asserts the we-ness of TV, the first-person plurality of taste within your social group. It builds a wall around the table; it asserts a private demographic. That's not conversation but its opposite." To a point, he's right, but Gerard and I find myriad points of interesting conflict to hash out during and after watching *Girls* and *Transparent*, for two relevant, recent, and provocative instances. If that dazzling repartee stays within our apartment, Engber would say, we're not changing anyone's mind or waging any impactful memes. But I maintain that it helps us to clarify how and what we think about issues and to take one more step on the road to enlightenment. And it manifests in how we interact with the people who live outside our apartment. And that obviously happens on a larger scale, aka social media. And there are a lot of smart people talking and writing about TV now, which was radically not the case even a decade ago. So Engber's argument is weakened in the face of this reality that is in large part a positive byproduct of the cyberverse. After a particular episode of HBO's *The Deuce*, for instance, I was itching to commune with someone about it and was able to do so on Twitter within five minutes. And I didn't even start the thread. It was there waiting for me. It was just what I needed—to be able to ask, "Is it just me, or was that porn scene directed by Candy really touching?" and have someone else respond, "Not just you. It was astonishing." This brief contact felt consequential, not at all like post-show "phatic" small talk that Engber attributes to typical dinner-party blabber. Evidence.

My consistent desire to talk smartly with smart people about TV leads me to wish for David Foster Wallace's perspective.

He was one of those thinker-writers who acknowledged the human enmeshment with and deep impact of TV on the modern human psyche. I had in mind for some time an ambitious project wherein I would comb all his writing for the TV bits, the way that actual literature scholars do with leitmotifs like water or lust.[1] Because it wasn't just in obvious places, like his essay "E unibus pluram: Television and U.S. Fiction," wherein he references both Sue Ann Nivens and Thomas Pynchon, or his short story "Little Expressionless Animals," where Alex Trebek and television itself have speaking parts, but it's sprinkled all over the place, including the door-stopping *Infinite Jest*, where he concocts the dystopian *Happy Days* marathons and product-sponsored years, the most memorable being the Year of the Depend Adult Undergarment; and his legendary "A Supposedly Fun Thing I'll Never Do Again," which is ostensibly an embedded observer's account of a cruise ship experience but actually, like TV, contains multitudes. Wallace was a creative, literary, freakishly intelligent person (and famously troubled soul whose posthumous reputation will be who-knows-where by the time this sentence is published) who obviously had deep and intricate thoughts about TV, just small but dense pieces that were colorful chips in his massive mosaics. I could say the same for Andy Warhol's creative output. In general, most of us think of TV as so much wallpaper, not worthy of mentioning as an entity that carries weight or has impact. Or we refer to it dismissively or jokingly as a vice the way we might do with coffee or alcohol, as if these aren't bona fide chemical substances affecting our brains. Maybe people like Warhol and Wallace saw TV differently, in fact, because of their interactions with said substances. I am vindicated by the knowledge that these artists thought about TV from ersatz-alien perspectives and shared those thoughts, even in the unheralded manner they did. More evidence.

Speaking of aliens, for fun I sometimes imagine that if I had to describe the evolution of TV to a Martian as succinctly as possible, I'd say: "TV is a method of advertising that uses entertaining programs that are beamed into pieces of furniture in people's homes to lure customers. But most viewers don't realize that and think the programs were made for them out of the goodness of the hearts of networks and studios. In the 1940s hardly anyone had a TV, but then people started getting them like crazy in the 1950s and 1960s. TV shows were mostly variety (*Your Show of Shows*, *The Ed Sullivan Show*, *Texaco Star Theater*), quiz shows (*Twenty-One*, *The $64,000 Question*, *Truth or Consequences*), situation comedies (*The Honeymooners*, *Leave It to Beaver*, *Father Knows Best*), and westerns (*The Lone Ranger*, *Gunsmoke*, *Bonanza*). People had three or four different programs they could choose from at any given time. They enjoyed it immensely—though a small sector believed it to be the downfall of society—and spent many hours watching it, often eating specially prepared one-tray meals in front of it. Then a different kind of system was invented where signals were sent through cables, and people subscribed and paid for it, but some people climbed on other people's roofs and somehow 'stole' 'cable' without the homeowners knowing or caring. The new system exponentially increased the number and type of programs that people could watch, including premium movies that people could hitherto see only in movie theaters or on big clunky tapes they played on a machine connected to the TV set with numerous confounding wires. Then the internet was, well, not invented, but available to the common human, and many more different ways of watching TV became available, but people didn't know if they should be calling it TV anymore, because it wasn't always watched on a thing called a TV set. A lot of people tried to call it 'content,' but 'TV' was tough to quit in more ways than one. Welcome to Earth, by the way!"

It so happens that this evolution is about a decade shy of paralleling my own. Mine was the first generation to grow up with the fact of TV, meaning we took it for granted, it was never a novelty, we couldn't imagine a world without it and so on, sort of like digital natives are to computers but arguably with less life-threatening dependence. TV was our window to the world, the way the internet is for kids (and other people) now, but with a much, much bigger pane. We could see the whole world on a screen from our couches. We couldn't interact with it the way we tend to do with computer screens, but we did in our own way. It was just as destructive and instructive as the WWW and yet, I think, more magical. Sometimes the more mechanical and explicit a machine, the more unfathomable it seems. Digital, cloud-based bits are easier to completely take for granted because they are effectively invisible. But how that unwieldy rotary phone apparatus and the associated wooden poles and wires outside allowed me to talk to someone a thousand miles away mystifies me more than email. While watching a close-up of a news teletype in action on a 1950-something-set episode of *The Crown*, for instance, Gerard clicked pause, looked at me pointedly, and said, "Someone invented that." Don't even get me started on the Pony Express, much less the pause button.

As I chronicle my half-century evolution, it will become clear that as much of an enthusiast as I may claim to be, I did not watch TV over the past fifty years strategically or wisely or with any forethought at all. I neglected seminal programs that are now commonly considered to be basic threads in our shared popular culture tapestry. "How can one consider oneself a true scholar without having read Proust?" a colleague once actually asked me rhetorically but seriously, not able to conceive that I have never once cracked the spine of *Swann's Way*. Similarly, how could I be taken seriously as a TV historian without having consumed *Star Trek*, *Twin Peaks*, *The Sopranos*, *The West Wing*, *The Wire*, and most of *The Simpsons*? I know I would have been all over *My So-Called Life* and *Freaks and Geeks* if I'd just been paying closer attention. But as it was, I never saw either one. If you're throwing down this book in disgust right now, I will not try to convince you to carry on. I have written people off for peccadillos far less egregious. I am half tempted to go back and watch all the episodes of everything I missed, but I have a day job and am not yet insane. As I often say—feel free to quote me—people know different things. Herein are the musings of a mere enthusiast, an ardent but imperfect one.

I have heard comedians and writers express disdain for their peers who rely too heavily on pop culture references, calling it lazy to pin their bits and tales to too specific a time period, rendering them shamefully dated and incomprehensible to different cultural groups or future generations. If you aspire to Twain- or Steinbeck-hood, maybe that's fair advice. But I don't expect any word in this book to end up on a page-a-day calendar. To wit, it is bursting with pop culture references, because sometimes specificity is the point. In part, then, I am deliberately and defiantly writing it for a slice of the populace. As you read, I hope you occasionally feel the same piercing joy that I did when writers Tina Fey, Robert Carlock, and Sam Means in an episode of *Unbreakable Kimmy Schmidt* had Carol Kane's neighborhood preservation activist Lillian shed a crocodile tear as she witnessed an urban hipster toss a can into a recycling bin, a twisted reference to the 1970s Keep America Beautiful campaign featuring the legendary crying Native American (the one later outed as Italian American). That *Kimmy* scene was for me, just me, a million of us thought as we laugh-cried separately-together. There are examples of this aplenty. In another one, in the Showtime sitcom *Happyish*, viewers learn via a calculated camera pan that the advertising firm where the protagonist toils, MGT, is the acronym for McMann Goldsmith Tate, an homage to McMann & Tate, the firm where *Bewitched*'s Darrin Stephens sold his mortal soul fifty years earlier. Just one more for now: In a season three episode of *The Good Place*, Ted Danson's otherworldly being beams himself back to Earth in the guise of a bartender, wiping a pint glass with a rag while smoothly dispensing life advice. Even though his hair was now white instead of brown, it was Sam Malone, and twenty-five years went poof. These incidents illustrate the private joke that, while incidental to the plot, panders to certain-aged viewers, reveals the sensibilities and nostalgia of the shows' writers, and may be designed to secure a loyal audience segment. That type of emotional manipulation is fine by me. Specificity, while inherently exclusive, has the power to insta-bond, like the construction worker who Krazy Glued his hard hat to an I-beam in the 1980 TV ad.

On the other hand, my periodic unabashed bingeing of *Raised by TV*, a podcast hosted by actor-comedians Lauren Lapkus and Jon Gabrus, taught me a valuable lesson. The idea of this show is so up my alley that it warrants a reserved parking spot. But I'm twenty years too old for it. Or am I? My wholehearted enjoyment of their show is an illustration of the universality of both TV passion and the medium's diasporic effects. Lapkus and Gabrus fashioned a totes adorbs, very profesh theme song for the show, parodying the manically cheerful style of all eighties and nineties sitcoms, then they proceed to "OMG!!" about every TV show, actor, commercial, and toy advertised on said commercial that comes to their minds, often while dialing up archival clips from YouTube, like an audio-only *Mystery Science Theater 3000* (a show these two are too young to have seen in its original run, much less be paying homage to). Even though I had only a passing familiarity with most of the shows and ads they were gleefully recalling—they seem especially fixated on *Full House*, which I surmise was the syndicated backdrop of their youth as *The Brady Bunch* was to mine—and was completely envious of their dewy youth but more so their performative, semipublic, likeminded TV gushing venture, I listened to episode after episode, fully on board with their enthusiastic nostalgia. Similarly, in the undergraduate class I teach about television, which I developed so I would have more people with whom to talk about TV, I find that these digital natives who never heard of *Who's the Boss*? can talk quite deeply about the programs they watch, and whether I watch the same ones or not, it is genuinely satisfying to me.

I was also digging the fact, the undeniable proof, the empirical evidence, that it is the medium that matters. I finally viscerally understood McLuhan—I think. The content is beside the point. Though it feels to the gusher that the content is the only thing that matters, the gusher is incapable of rational thought given that her judgment is clouded by pleasure. It's not *Three's Company* or the singing-spelling Oscar Mayer bologna boy. It's the memory of that thing, enhanced by the simultaneous collective remembering. It's a nostalgia orgy. And I derive pleasure just by observing from the sidelines, remembering my own remembering. Take heed, communications theory, sociology, and philosophy professors. You should be leaping on this opportunity for at least one class session analyzing this tableau. McLuhan, Halbwachs, and Bob Saget in the same lecture may help perk up the ears of your students who might otherwise be looking at their phones. In sum, it's both specificity (aka content, aka the message)—which brings instant gratification, and medium—which is the delivery system that allows it to happen. This must be how Stephen Hawking felt when coming up with the singularity theorems.

Regardless of the era or the content, for anyone who watched TV throughout a lifetime, it has to be given some credit for shaping that life. It provides a frame around personal pushpins, and in the aggregate, our testimonies make up generational, cultural, historical documentation. I am exercising the audacity to record my journey, reasoning that it's a shared one. What gives me courage is the very idea that what I have experienced is not unique, but rather the very definition of common. When I told a friend recently that I was writing a personal reflection of television, she laughed and said, actually aloud, "Well, *I* could do *that*!" Instead of lunging at the low-hanging reply, "Well, you're not, are you?" I was reminded of the writer Leslie Jamison, who in her memoir, *The Recovering: Intoxication and Its Aftermath*, strenuously disabused herself and her readers of her specialness. She was clearly concerned with facing her own and others' "disdain for the already-told story" and warding off accusations of putting out "just another addiction memoir." Here's the part I am coopting for my purposes: ". . . a story's sameness is precisely why it should be told. Your story is only useful because others have lived it and will live it again." Not to liken my tales to an addiction narrative (though the word "addiction" is lavishly applied in relation to electronic media consumption nowadays), but Jamison's assertion applies to any shared experience, good or bad.

The first two books I wrote about TV served the purposes of 1) distraction from existential dread and 2) successful completion of tenure and promotion requirements as a faculty member, a role that came with my librarian job the way a sunny top-floor apartment comes with a six-flight walk-up.

Pertaining to the latter, "what kind of adult career consists of a combination of scholastic drudgery and entertainment—the dutiful churning out of book reports about stuff that everyone else does for fun?" asks *New York Times* film critic A. O. Scott in his 2016 book *Better Living through Criticism*. Hello! This kind. If I had to produce *this* book as a product of scholarship, I'd call it an autoethnography and frequently use the requisite gratuitous phrases "textual analysis" and "the ways in which." In fact, when I told a faculty colleague only my working title, she saw my game straight away: "Oooh. Autotheory around the psychological impact of *Match Game '76*?" You got it! But with more emphasis on the "auto" and none of the actual theory. (As for *Match Game*, it was one of the many 1970s offerings that left me with the impression that adults were continuously drunk and horny, a feeling about which I was ambivalent but mostly just comfortable and left emotionally unscathed.) Unlike my other two books, this one does not have endnotes or an index or a compulsive reiterating of an "argument" beyond what I have already stated as the thesis. Some sentences are grammatically incomplete, and neologisms are employed when regular words just won't do. It's not actual social science, because I did not take deliberate and copious notes about my experience since age four. Like Margaret Mead, I lived among the natives and, unlike Mead, I was genuinely one of them. I realize that its dead-center target audience (my generational peers) may be a relatively narrow slice, but there are a lot of us. I am far from the only person to grow up on TV, and that is exactly why I wrote this book about ourselves.

More than a collective trip down memory lane, I hope this is a testament to the inescapable effect of TV on the life of a person and consequently, a generation and by overgeneralization, a culture, a nation, and the human race. What it is not is the written equivalent of *Saturday Night Live*'s "The Chris Farley Show," where the fawning Farley would address his guest, say Jeff Daniels, with "Remember in *Die Hard* when Bruce Willis had to walk on all the broken glass barefoot? Did you like that? Me, too. That was awesome." I mean, remember "The Chris Farley Show?" That was awesome. But that particular format is not really sustainable, writing-wise or reading-wise. It's also about another universal truism, and that's how we think about a particular art form (or cultural product, or anything, really) and how, if we continue to stay in touch with our own minds, how our thinking about it changes over time. I am also not coming at you à la *Dream On*'s Martin Tupper, where I show you a lot of parallels between my life and TV plots from the past, even though I could easily do so with *The Brady Bunch* and *Seinfeld* alone. As could you.

It is also not a memoir, per se, though there is no fitting word for what it is, so I might use that word occasionally. This book is one part indulgent personal history and two parts a professional coming-of-age story. If you are still with me despite my ignorance about *Freaks and Geeks*, you might wish to quit now, because I'm warning you that I do not reveal the heartbreaking inner demons or saucy exploits that you have surely come to enjoy reading about in other people's life stories. There is one of the latter, but really that was the only one that happened to me, and it's hardly saucy. I have already mentioned my husband, and he will come up again, but there is no emotional agony there either. Gerard called me for a first date—we met via mutual friends—during the commercial breaks between *Friends* and *Will & Grace*, whether by intention or kismet, and you can discern all you need to know from that.

My TV imperial phase was the 1970s. The conventional TV history wisdom, the stuff of A&E documentaries, coffee table books and encyclopedias, would have TV's golden age as the 1950s, the days of *Playhouse 90* and Carnegie Hall telecasts. TV critic Matt Zoller Seitz who, in arguing for 1980s TV as foundational to the quality TV we enjoy thirty years later, astutely calls out "recency bias—the fallacy that whatever artistic developments you happened to grow up with represent the Greatest of All Time." I know a lot of people who would say the only thing golden about 1980s TV was *The Golden Girls*. These people are mostly recency bigots from my age cohort. The 1980s were Seitz's golden age, and the 1970s were mine (and ipso facto, the 1970s were the Greatest of All Time). Bob Thompson, director of the Bleier Center for Television & Popular Culture at Syracuse University wrote a book called *Television's Second Golden Age: From Hill Street Blues to ER*. The phase we are in as I write this is a period that many are referring to as TV's third golden age, though some say it's only the second, some are adamant that it is the first true one, and others hedge by simply referring to it as the "new golden age." Not as clearly delineated as the waves of feminism and, some would argue, not as critical, golden dating is clearly an exercise in subjectivity. It seems obvious that every era is someone's golden age. One person's trash is another's treasure. Good and bad stuff have always and will always coexist.

To grease the wheels of memory, I have watched countless YouTube clips that led to more shows from the era that I had forgotten about. I would also ask friends if they remembered certain things, and then they'd remind me of other things. This book heavily favors sitcoms ("the defining commercial art form of the 20th century" per *New York Times* culture writer Sam Anderson) over dramas. And by no means do I cover everything I watched, not even every show that mattered to me. There's too much. Some of the programs or moments that I cover in here will be quirky particulars that will hopefully be shared remembrances with at least a couple of you. Others will be the TV milestones, the greatest hits, the TV events that, even after the splintered era of cable and several dozen other delivery systems, everybody at least knew about. They were newsworthy for reasons that tell us something about us—not always a flattering something, but something worth knowing.

So if I don't mention *New Zoo Revue* and that incenses you, write your own, be mad, feel bad for me, but for god sakes don't be one of those tiresome people who vituperates about it in an Amazon review. This is a work of entertaining ideas (a phrase that can be understood in two ways, both apt), not a reference book. Though the *idea* of a comments section turning into a subreddit nostalgia party on everybody's favorite TV show would be gratifying.

As a convalescing academic, I hope this book will entertain both my peers in media and pop culture studies as well as anyone who ever enjoyed watching TV. For the former it should be like a play date and for the latter some validation for all your own TV watching. I've found it to be true that too many years of writing like an academic can impair the ability to write like a regular person, much less rediscover one's own voice. Mortarboard hat head can be more stubborn than ring around the collar, scrubbing and soaking to no avail. I'm unable to squelch my strong desire to fact check and look down side roads. I cannot resist research tangents, both because it's a procrastination device that doesn't feel as craven as post-breakfast napping or chain watching baby goat videos and because I love looking stuff up. For ten years I've been writing things that are put under scrutiny by that anonymous group of sadists known as peer reviewers, who come back with comments like "So-and-so's theory of something-something is not mentioned here, nor does it reflect on the critical impact of this and that. Publication recommended with substantial, nearly-impossible-without-turning-it-into-something-completely-different revisions." Or "It is difficult to see what new knowledge is being created here. This is merely descriptive. Publication not recommended." I never really understood what the problem was with being descriptive, but I think it's the equivalent of "super dumb" in the world of scholarship. I want to go back to comfortably describing, and it's not that easy. I try to ignore the voice that says I need to read—really read, not just cite passages from—Bourdieu's *Taste* before writing this book, or even the much shorter and more accessible *Celine Dion's Let's Talk about Love: A Journey to the End of Taste* by music critic Carl Wilson. That all said, I do insert historical and cultural context here and there throughout this romp, when called for or when I feel like it, but I have done my best to keep secondary research to a minimum and have utterly banned section headings. The effort required in that restraint, however, is a clue that I am still not entirely rehabilitated.

The arc of my journey with TV starts with a heavy, wood-veneer, cathode ray Sylvania television set, manufactured in the early 1960s, atop of which sat a set of rabbit-ear antennae and the side of which withstood untold accounts of corporal abuse for vexatious horizontal picture lines. That beast offered four watchable channels. One version of the narrative could have the arc ending when I donated my late twentieth- century, nineteen-inch Panasonic to the Salvation Army in 2008—the last television set I would ever own. Another version, and the one that is more accurate, puts that TV-set-liberating moment at the apex of the arc. I am now somewhere on the descending segment, in some golden age or another, frequently binge-watching "content" on numerous devices, the largest of those smaller than a breadbox.

A parallel arc, or perhaps more appropriately, a proverbial full circle, illustrates the evolving role of TV in my life, transformed from something seemingly purposeless and mundane into something meaningful and a source of pride and unabashed pleasure. My story, resting largely on memory as the primary source data, is evidence that TV matters. After having pressed my TV love into academic service, helping me get up those six flights of stairs, I'm grateful to return to it with feeling as well as the wider lens it deserves.

NOTE

1. Of course, someone already took on that project, so I don't have to. In *The Gospel According to David Foster Wallace: Boredom and Addiction in an Age of Distraction*, there is no one chapter called "TV," but it's woven throughout, as TV is wont to be. This is the only endnote that will appear in this book, an homage to DFW.

1

In the Beginning

On a Monday morning in June 1965, my mother was not watching *I Love Lucy*, an activity far more leisurely than the one she was engaged in, which was giving birth to me. She probably would have even preferred seeing trimnastics with Jack LaLanne or Vice President Hubert Humphrey expound on US foreign policy, which were also on the air as she was pushing me out in a Lamaze-free milieu. Later that day, there was a plethora of game shows to choose from—*Truth or Consequences*, *The Price Is Right*, *Password*; talk shows—*Girl Talk: Virginia Graham*, *Art Linkletter's House Party*; soaps—*The Guiding Light*, *The Secret Storm*, *The Doctors*; lots of news programs; full-on movies in broad weekday light, including *The Boy with the Green Hair*, about a bullied war orphan played by a preteen Dean Stockwell, and *Betrayed Women*, a 1948 drama about a women's prison. At the end of that exhausting and life-giving day, if Mom was up for it, during prime time she might have chosen from *I've Got a Secret*, the panel game show hosted by Steve Allen, *The Man from U.N.C.L.E.*, *The Andy Griffith Show*, or *The Honeymooners*.

The TV planet onto which I emerged might well have been in another universe, it was that different from the one onto which any given baby is born on any given Monday as I write this some fifty years on. Among the few options a viewer had on that June 1965 evening were the network offerings of the lively, star-studded *Andy Williams Show* or *The Danny Thomas Show*; or a viewer could go highbrow with the public broadcasting option of William F. Buckley debating James Baldwin on "the American Dream—has it been achieved at the expense of the American Negro?" There was the gamut, right there, something for everybody, if by "something" we mean a quite possibly ill-fitting program and by "everybody" we include a potentially apathetic viewer (or, per the laws of probability, in many cases a perfect match). Even so, you didn't hear people whining, "There's nothing on!" There was plenty, more than enough, and most were grateful and delighted. But I romanticize the yesteryears—intellectual debates popping up in prime time and Edward R. Murrow documentaries and British drama imports right there, unavoidable, in plain sight. But it was not all book discussions and classical music appreciation, lest we forget *The Beverly Hillbillies* and *My Favorite Martian*. These sitcoms got the eyeballs. And because TV was a relatively new culturally threatening upstart in the middle of the twentieth century, detractors at the time focused on the insipid, referring to the piece of furniture as the "idiot box" and the array of programming as a "wasteland." Perhaps until very recently, TV has continued to be reflexively referred to as lowbrow rubbish. But grocery stores have baby kale as well as Cool Ranch Doritos, and we don't call the supermarket a "junk food building."

Televisual content (henceforth shorthanded as TV, albeit technically inaccurate in many cases) has mushroomed, and there is a lot more good stuff and a lot more junk. One could argue that we are in a more liberal place in the early twenty-first century because people watch shows for all different kinds of reasons. Consider, for instance, the existence of "hate watching." Indeed, we are less likely to feel or express shame and embarrassment about watching certain shows, and there is so much to consume—now there really is something for everyone—but you could argue even more convincingly that we are in a more confining space. While the same viewer who watched *The Honeymooners* in 1965 may well have watched the decidedly different-toned Buckley/Baldwin debate, she may have done so because there were far fewer screentime options, and she'd rather watch something than nothing; or maybe "hate watching" has always been a thing. Fifty years ago she would likely be passively consuming what was presented to her, whereas now she is installed in her media viewing bubble, proactively watching on demand whatever she wants. We think of the latter as technological progress, but—and here I go romanticizing again—I think it was the former that was magical. I'm nostalgic for the idea that a Ralph Kramden fan might serendipitously be introduced to the racial ideologies of the author of *Notes of a Native Son*, simply because she didn't feel like hauling herself off to bed.

The TV lineup on my first day of life was a pretty good bellwether for the era. I'm just mystical-minded enough to believe I might discover a clue from the TV universe I was born into that, in addition to my genetic material, explains me to myself. It sounds like hooey, I know, because I couldn't have watched with any kind of cognizance for a few more years, but I was in the room when others watched it and absorbed my parents' and grandparents' and various other adults' reactions to what was going on in the world and therefore on television. After the racial politics discussion on public broadcasting, a viewer could get up off the couch and switch the channel to escape via *The Alfred Hitchcock Hour* or wallow in some more Sturm und Drang with "The Berkeley Rebels," a special report from *CBS News with Harry Reasoner* about the UC Berkeley anti-establishment student activists. "You don't need any ideology to say that the society stinks!" said the promo for that special report in the newspaper TV listings. And that Reasoner special was not a one-off. What I was watching at the Paley Center that hot summer weekday was more in the same vein. On June 28, 1965, DJ Murray the K hosted a network special, *It's What's Happening, Baby*, sponsored by the bygone US Office of Economic Opportunities promoting its New Chance program—which hoped to nudge young people toward economic self-sufficiency—with a smorgasbord of big-name entertainers like the Temptations, Tom Jones, Ray Charles, Martha and the Vandellas, Marvin Gaye, the Dave Clark Five, the Supremes, and at least a dozen more. The kids were wild about it. Conservative congressmen, not so much. Later on, Murray's camp claimed to have inaugurated the concept of the music video with that broadcast. What is certain is that the program telegraphed a national issue in a bouncier manner than a history textbook or Wikipedia page would.

The real world and mine continued to coexist on parallel tracks with me mostly oblivious. As it happened, in fact, just days before the Apollo 12 moonwalk and the My Lai Massacre were announced on the network evening news in November 1969, history was being made over in the neighborhood where Mr. Fred McFeely Rogers had put down roots the previous year. I was there on the ground floor of *Sesame Street*'s debut, an early adopter, and a strong supporter from day one, if support can be measured in unblinking fixation. Its debut in the midst of the Vietnam War and the civil rights movement was no coincidence; the show's creators were politically liberal advocates of television's educational and activist potential. Thanks to the Children's Television Workshop, I learned to count to twenty in Spanish before I got to first grade and was introduced to diversity and creativity and the hippest of entertainers long before I would have otherwise. It was all so friendly and active and fun and education by stealth—how could that not have a prosocial effect on a mass scale? Of course it did, and there are piles of research to prove it, but a) I am not here to support my argument with hard evidence, and b) aren't anecdotal testimonies more convincing anyway?

I came up in a groovy era, for better or worse. Things that are now categorized as child abuse or neglect were, in the 1960s and 1970s, not given concern. Kids' domestic existence approximated that of indoor-outdoor pets. Seatbelts and an actual nutritious breakfast (not just a Pop-Tart sprinkled with colored sugar and trace vitamins and minerals) were rarely exercised options; we could stay alone in the car while our parents went into the store; bike helmets were worn only by (some) adults and only on motorcycles. And we sat mere inches away from the TV set, so close that our hair statically clung to the screen, crackling wondrously. I'm certain a passing adult occasionally admonished me, but I didn't heed, and she would be out of the room before the words "ruin your eyes" had passed the cigarette attached to her lip.

There were a lot of things we citizens of that devil-may-care era weren't afraid of that we should have been—first- and second-hand smoke, saccharine, the sun, Diethylstilbestrol, Bill Cosby—but also a battery of threats that gave me nightmares, terrifying scenarios of which no reasonable arguments could disabuse me. I was convinced that upon entering middle school, the "drug pushers" that my parents blithely, in my presence, tsk-tsked about with their friends would push me against the lockers and shove pills down my throat (thank you, anonymous author of *Go Ask Alice*). Any time my parents visited boat-owning friends who lived near the ocean, I waited in a state of heightened agitation for the news from my godparents that Mom and Dad had been chomped to their gory death by a shark (Spielberg, you devil!). The now-legendary Double Initial Murderer was on a spree in 1973 in Rochester, New York, and guess where I lived? I was genuinely concerned not only for the safety of my friends Marybeth Miller and Susan Scheff but even more so for my own potential gruesome demise—how would I be spared by this insane criminal who was most assuredly choosing victims based only on phonetics?

Even though the lurking of the alphabet psychopath and all the other sensational bad news was brought to me by television, I didn't hate the messenger. Not even when we were subjected to a blood-curdling test of the Emergency Broadcast System. I don't even want to think about what my mom told me *that* was for. I loved TV with all my heart and soul. Nothing could tear us asunder. The positive far outweighed the negative. Besides, most of the content I consumed was of the kid-friendly variety, offered up in a safe, day-lit timeslot or publicly funded zone and blissfully above the fray of the real world.

Weekday mornings consisted of TV time as the sun rose, before we drove my dad to work, my mom's pink hair tape still holding her damp curls in place. I was supremely fond of *Captain Kangaroo* and *Romper Room* and had less room in my heart for *Underdog*, *Tennessee Tuxedo*, and *The Adventures of Rocky and Bullwinkle*. Inexplicably, animation never sustained my attention (and never could—a crippling character weakness for when *The Simpsons* came around). Even though I am almost certain the cartoons, especially the Mel Blanc, Looney Tunes variety, were innovative and clever, given that they contained subliminal literary references, I always leaned more toward the live-action types—*The Lost Saucer, Sigmund and the Sea Monsters, H. R. Pufnstuf. The Jetsons* and *The Flintstones* were exceptions (and much later Comedy Central's *Dr. Katz, Professional Therapist* and much, much later *BoJack Horseman* and Bill Burr's *F Is for Family*). These two were a class apart in my mental hierarchy. Maybe it was the space age and prehistoric settings, respectively, that made me feel like I was watching something approaching a movie, which overrode the juvenile animation. Would that I was attracted to the proto-MOOC, *Sunrise Semester*—who knows what variety of genius grants I would be boasting now? But I don't recall ever laying eyes on the thing, so resentful was I of the very unintelligible, un-fun-sounding phrase taking up valuable space in the TV listings, not to mention on the air.

The Art Clokey claymation joints were also in a separate column. *The Gumby Show* and *Davey and Goliath* mesmerized me simply for their visual appeal. I enjoyed these clay figures, I believe, for the same reasons I enjoyed pre-cable cooking shows—they were slow and earnest, and suggested interesting textures. The content of these two series, however, I eschewed or forgot. I was no stranger to tuning out religious indoctrination—I attended CCD (indoctrination for public school Catholic kids) every week until I was confirmed at age thirteen—and I could not abide Davey's treacly, goody-goodyness. The fact that it was probably relatively progressive—they had a couple of brown clay kids in it—was lost on me. Gumby did not likewise bombard with morality, and though I remember nothing of the plots, I was happy to own my own Gumby and Pokey facsimiles, whose real-life tactile consistency was only mildly satisfying. It's not insignificant that these programs aired on the weekend, the bastion of endless cartoons. I gave Scooby and the Road Runner some attention—an animal lover early on—but for the most part I spent Saturday mornings away from the TV, probably engaged in a superior, mind-expanding activity, like pressing Silly Putty into the comics page or trying to get the Slinky to behave on my own staircase the way it did on the commercial.

Overall, in the genre of children's programming, I preferred shows that weren't complete kidocracies. I understand that it was supposed to be empowering and freeing for minors to be in charge with no specter of buzz-killing adults, but it made me uncomfortable. If there was at least some adult presence—Fran (of the she, Kukla, and Ollie trio), Miss Rita on *Romper Room*—I could relax. Rita Moreno and Morgan Freeman gave credence to the kid-tastic aura of *The Electric Company*. *Sesame Street* always had a Maria, Luis, or Mr. Hooper showing up on the reg. It felt safer, neater, more controlled. I didn't like being part of something where the inmates were running the asylum. Grown-ups (and select animals and puppets) classed up the joint, and I also had a hunch that they understood me better than my peers did.

I didn't know from public or commercial stations at this juncture, but I did feel an inchoate comfort in PBS land. As an impressionable youth being brainwashed by "state-sponsored leftism," "viewers like me" were being groomed for nostalgia-driven financial as well as political support later on. That boy has been crying wolf almost continually since the inception of the Corporation for Public Broadcasting in 1967, and each time it seems like the real deal—the end of public broadcasting. "Viewers like me" find ourselves conscripted cyclically, frantically sending effortless and likely ineffectual precomposed emails to our legislators, though we are unable to remember the last time we donated to our local station. To add insult to injury, in a controversial but seemingly swift transaction, *Sesame*

Street moved out of its flagship public neighborhood in 2016 and into the most coveted real estate of all at the time—HBO. Controversial because the gates of that neighborhood required an entrance fee, the antithesis of the welcoming, even basic cableness of PBS. While I haven't really watched *Sesame Street* in about forty years, the movin' on up felt like a betrayal and a significant loss, akin to finding out your favorite elementary school teacher gave up teaching for a career in finance.

For so many of us, Big Bird was synonymous with public broadcasting, but there were a lot of other reasons I spent my time watching my local WXXI, channel 21, too. While I went through most of my youth overtly disdaining Mister Rogers—he was as uncool as the adults on *Sesame Street* were cool—I watched his show in tandem with Cookie Monster et al. and was particularly fond of Picture Picture, with its mesmerizing factory mini-docs, and had a secret crush on Handyman Negri. The trolley's bell, as it appeared on that enviable shelf above the enviable window seat, did not, in fact, make me roll my eyes but was a Pavlovian amuse-bouche. I was not above getting excited about seeing what Donkey Hodie, Daniel Striped Tiger, and my meow-meow girl Henrietta Pussycat were up to in the Neighborhood of Make-Believe, though I was precocious enough to realize that was too prosaic a name for such a wackadoodle place. It was most certainly thanks to that infernal trolley that I nursed a years-long daydream of being able to ride a moving sidewalk from my backyard all the way to Paris. Mister Rogers would smile gently in agreement at this but would not take the credit for sparking my imagination, instead telling me that I'm special, thereby instilling a base of self-esteem that really can, in part, be traced back to him. I owe him some credit, too, for my penchant for cardigans—oh, and humanitarian ethics.

Hodgepodge Lodge was a program that could have been a parody of public broadcasting, and I am reasonably certain it was shown only on my TV, and even I was not a regular, despite the fact that it was on for seven years. It was hosted by a naturalist in her fifties called Miss Jean, who seemed to live alone in a cabin in the woods. She had little children over and proceeded to talk to them very quietly in a Mister Rogers sort of way about nature things. Just as *Sesame Street* was meant as a mirror for city kids, so *Hodgepodge* was designed to introduce those city kids to nature. I grew up in the suburbs, and much of it was news to me, too. Even though there was an adult present, and even though she was a harmless middle-aged lady, I did not feel exactly safe the way I did on *Sesame Street*, where there were plenty of people around and places to hide if something went awry. I still feel more fearful in the country than in the city. But I also find, now that I am Miss Jean's age, that I prefer the company of trees and wildlife to most people. So I suspect she might take some credit for that.

Unlike *Hodgepodge*, *Zoom*—strictly kidocratic, but I was nevertheless seduced—had a lasting effect on me and on my peers. For starters, Ubbi Dubbi was what Esperanto wanted to be in terms of mass adoption. Also, an unusually large swath of Americans pointlessly knows one Boston area zip code. I added to the burden of the mailroom when I sent a postcard to Box 350 requesting the American Sign Language alphabet card. If you're keeping a tally, you will note that thanks to WXXI, I had learned the basics of three languages in addition to my native one before I even began my lifelong affair with French in a brick-and-mortar school. On *Zoom*, I also learned, in theory, how to make an operational raft using Styrofoam blocks and venetian blinds. But the most enduring legacy for me and every single girl in my middle school was Bernadette's maneuver, best described as an intertwining baton twirl of the forearms. *Zoom* might also have provoked the first of many fashion trends I mindlessly followed—the striped rugby shirt—that did my pale face and gender-neutral hairstyle no favors.

I didn't know what the entity of public broadcasting was, but I sensed that it was somehow different from the commercial networks, with their vivid, shouty ads and local interstitials—"Dialing for Dollars" and surreal spots for the local, though "world's largest," guitar store, House of Guitars (my Rochester brothers and sisters will count Eddie Meath among their time capsule gems, with his penny fund and gentle "quiet money" requests). Because much of my afterschool watching was on public broadcasting and took place at my Grandma Deedle's, I associated that programming with her house. She and Grandpa Shrink (a psychiatrist) had wall-to-wall carpeting in every single of the many rooms of a four-bedroom split-level with a finished basement (including full bar). My educational TV watching took place in the "porch," a renovated formerly screened-in area transformed by wood paneling and a plush goldenrod colored carpet into an ersatz genie's bottle, with more plaid and La-Z-Boy and no Persian inflection and zero tufted ottomans. I was left to my devices, sitting too close. The atmosphere at this house was quiet and high-toned. No stereo speakers rigged into the essential rooms, just a radio playing state-sponsored leftism in the kitchen, which was usually proselytizing at no one. I was occasionally aware of the sound of rummaging in the ice bucket, which contrasted with the distant sound of the opening of a Schlitz pull tab at home. Even though the network channels were available on Grandma's porch TV, I don't remember ever watching them there. Everything felt different at Grandma Deedle's, the way eating a Nestlé Crunch bar outside in the cold always tasted different—not better, just different—from eating it inside. I was equally comfortable and felt like myself in both homes.

2

Off-Label TV

Bad news and evil talking trees notwithstanding, I found everything about television comforting. As an only child, I had, for many hours of the day, complete control of the dial. When I was forced to watch *Batman* or *Emergency!* at friends' homes because an older (usually boy) sibling dominated, and I was not self-possessed enough to go off to a corner to read, I felt cold and homesick. Like animation, shows that revolved around action and male-oriented premises did nothing for me. I wasn't afraid of or squeamish or morally opposed to gratuitous violence, just bored. As with a cat looking in the mirror, the image just did not register. I needed something that resembled life as I knew it to get me sucked in.

My preferences fell along the family sitcom continuum. The two that spring to mind, coincidentally and immaterially, featured nontraditional families. Both *Family Affair* and *The Courtship of Eddie's Father* proffered unwed, male parent figures as protagonists. (Though on *Family Affair*, Uncle Bill's valet, Mr. French, [un]naturally took the brunt of the childcare, and Mrs. Livingston was the equivalent sidekick for "Mr. Eddie's

Father.") *Family Affair* was also the source of the oddly coveted Mrs. Beasley doll, in her unflattering oversized polka dots, granny glasses, and coarse hair devoid of color. How many kids today clamor for an elderly lady doll in Walmart?

But my tastes, like my inherited but unrequited faith, were catholic. I was also a devotee of *Gilligan's Island*, *The Brady Bunch*, *My Three Sons*, *Room 222*, and *Love, American Style*. While I'm still not sure who the target audience was for some of these shows—I have to believe that laugh tracks were employed out of desperation to counteract the broadness of the humor—I know for sure that *Laugh-In* was not for the 5–8-year-old demographic. Even though 99.9 percent of the show's irreverent, politically and sexually charged humor was above my head, how was a kid to resist the visual appeal of Lily Tomlin's Edith Ann in her giant rocking chair or Judy Carne's Sock It to Me Girl or Flip Wilson as Geraldine, I ask you? The naughty bits may as well have been uttered in Mandarin, they were so outside of my comprehension zone. I would like to use this as proof for the family-values zealots that what I didn't take in couldn't scar me, but how would that square with giving credit where it's due vis-à-vis my lifetime devotion to irreverent humor?

While I may not have been the sought-after audience for *Laugh-In*, the show's delivery style spoke directly to my ilk. As uber-*Jeopardy* champion, polymath, and writer Ken Jennings notes in his book *Planet Funny: How Comedy Took Over Our Culture*, "The ad world was the first industry to learn that humor was a reliable way to increase the attention, comprehension, and persuasion of just about any audience. Then *Sesame Street* brought the same approach to the world of education, teaching generations of children letters and numbers using the 1960s sketch comedy playbook of *Laugh-In*." I fancy myself being the only 5–8-year-old who was a fan of both shows, but given the generally accepted TV-as-babysitter era and my narcissistic worldview, of course that can't be true. On a related note about laugh tracks, most of us find them annoying and lowbrow to our prestige-conditioned ears, but they may have had an off-label effect. On a 2018 episode of the *Decoder Ring* podcast, audio editor and laugh track nerd Paul Iverson reminisced about laugh tracks on his favorite shows when he was a kid. "There's people watching with me," he said. "And they sound like adults. They don't sound like children." I am certain hearing the laughter produced a communal feeling for me, too, and subconsciously made me feel fine—even sophisticated—about watching adult-themed shows.

Though I tended toward the more interpersonal and less action-packed programming, I found the idea of TV itself exciting. The technology thrilled me. The set of my formative years was a huge, hot, heavy box. It was of the variety known as a console TV and at one time was probably de rigueur in American middle-class homes. Ours was not the super-heavy anvil type with sculpted mahogany Italianate detail that was flush with the floor and would not or could not be moved for decades, like a piano, around which furniture was arranged for at least two generations. In comparison ours was more mid-century modern but only because the wood was relatively light and sat atop short, angled legs. If one wanted to rearrange the furniture in our den, which happened a few times, it would require my father and the next-door husband and lots of sweating and a few beers. What I can recall with intense tactile detail is the milky greenish-brown plastic channel knobs and the smaller metal-ridged knob for fine tuning. The materials of those last two should have been reversed based on frequency of use and potential wear and tear. I can yet conjure up the feeling of tension in my right hand when grasping that plastic ridge and feeling it give just the slightest bit, always fearing it would break and then pliers would be required to live on top of the TV to do the job, and so much of the pleasure of TV watching would be sucked away. What a satisfying action, manually heaving from one channel and clunking over into the next, making you feel as though you really were going into a new land or at least a new neighborhood.

Channel flipping was the most common action perpetrated upon the television, followed closely by whumping its side for a variety of emotional expressions masked as "technical" adjustments to force horizontal lines into submission. I was forever being reprimanded for flipping the channel too fast. I had developed the muscle memory of performing a nonstop flight from 13 (ABC) to 8 (NBC), but when my father witnessed this well-honed technique, he told me I was ruining the tube. And he was not invoking the affectionate shorthand for television, but the sprocket that powered the whole operation and delivered unconditional joy to my daily life. So, I learned to methodically move from channel to channel, bobbing my head with a showy annoyance as I rested on each unnecessary channel for a nanosecond—at least when he was in eyeshot. But that silver knob—who ever used it? What was it for? It finely tuned *bupkis*. That was what the banging was for. And despite my father's warning about the destructive channel flipping, he was our household's banger-in-chief. On top of the set were the rabbit-ear antennae, two thin metal poles projecting from a plastic base that were ultimately, like the shiny fine tuner, merely decorative. There was also a Chianti bottle gifted to us by my crafty aunt, which she had transformed into a candleholder collaged with bits of masking tape then rubbed with a burnt sienna shoe polish. And though this may have happened only once, I know the top of the enormous energy-sucking and heat-emitting TV was also an excellent place to activate a tiny clear plastic box of Mexican jumping beans.

As in so many American homes, from the 1950s onward, the room with the TV in it was the TV Room. In our house, it was just The Den, but the purpose was implicit. The only objects larger than the TV in the room were an upright piano, a convertible red Naugahyde couch, and a braided oval area rug. Four collapsible TV tables, thin aluminum trays on wobbly aluminum legs, were stored on a rolling rack in the den closet and were trotted out for rare, special occasion viewings, like the annual broadcast of *The Wizard of Oz* or me getting to eat a TV dinner. Years later, I saw the Conner family using a mirror image of these tables on *Roseanne*, and I started to draw a bunch of conclusions based on social class and then quickly nipped that dreamy academic pursuit in the bud.

Nothing presaged a TV tray opportunity like my mother appliqued with sky blue eye shadow, floating in a cloud of Shalimar, and my dad sporting a Dry Look look and a sharp leather blazer. As they prepped for their night out—often for something called a "dinner dance," which sounded like a punishment to me—I anticipated the babysitter's arrival and preheated the oven for my TV dinner. It was always a toss-up between Libbyland and Swanson. Swanson offered far better quality—I had no problem consuming a Hungry Man Salisbury steak dinner (always a gifted eater, I regularly scored two Big Macs when with my grandmother because she didn't enjoy my company as much when I was "irritable"), but Libbyland was whimsical *fun*. After downing the contents of each compartment, I was rewarded with an embossed likeness of one of the Libbyland characters, Libby's (they of the "on the label label label" company) madcap take on Billy the Kid and his associates. The taste of the Libbyland kid-friendly hot dog and fish stick meals was godawful, but it came with puzzles, a pop-up backdrop, and chocolate milk in a pouch. Libbyland was around only for the first half of the 1970s, and until the internet I was convinced I had imagined it, because I have yet to find one real-life person who remembers it. When I look at the retro enthusiasts' images of the mini meatballs drowning in orange-red sauce, I can taste it taste it taste it, and I do not like it like it like it.

The Wizard of Oz usually appeared in the TV schedule around Easter, and I would begin pestering my mother early in March to make sure we didn't miss it (the ultimate instance of appointment viewing)—because not only did I never know when Easter was going to happen (I still don't), but in 1973 if we missed it, we would have to wait another year-ish until it reappeared. Though *Wizard* was an Academy Award–nominated film classic and not a TV show or even a Movie of the Week, I never saw it anywhere but on a TV screen. And the fact that we had only a black-and-white TV for the first decade of my life, thereby making the second half of the famously color-centric Technicolor movie lose a little something, made absolutely no difference to me. I'm sure when I finally first saw the movie in color a few years later, I was no more delighted than I was watching it while eating—on the celebratory TV tray tables—the ritual Jell-O golden egg custard with nutmeg served in whisky glasses with the gold band around the equator.

It's likely unnecessary to say that the den was where I clocked the most hours, but while I was monitored for speed of channel flipping, this was not the case for the content or the length of time spent watching it. In case it's not clear as crystal by this point, I watched a lot of TV. One late weekend afternoon, I was livid with my mother, who was snack blocking because it was close to alleged dinnertime. I took one of my china tea set plates, stomped past her in the kitchen to go out to the backyard to wretchedly tear up some of the lawn to put on the plate, stomped past her in the kitchen again, making sure she saw what I must resort to in order to fend off starvation, and then stomped to the den and slammed the door so hard it stuck. My dad stormed down the hall, preparing to take a swift left into the room to berate me for such impudence, but he couldn't open the door no matter what he tried or how loudly or vilely he swore. When I realized they—my now-hysterical mother, apoplectic father, and the next-door husband—were on the case, I put my anxiety temporarily aside. Trapped in the room with the TV? Sign me up. I dumped the passive-aggressive amuse-bouche of grass out the window and settled in to enjoy *Winnie the Pooh and the Blustery Day* while the crew figured out how to remove the door from its hinges. Via the power of self-preservation, whatever occurred after the door liberation is erased from memory.

I wasn't always alone or with other kids in front of the TV. While the set was essentially my domain during the daylight hours, my parents had control during prime time. This duo was far from anti-TV or public-TV snobs and spent their fair share of time ordering me to change the channel for them from their seat of authority six feet from the screen. We had one TV, and if they wanted to watch something, their preference carried. But I was not excessively discerning. Except for news or sports—which when they came on I would take to my room and practice the *M*A*S*H* theme song, "Suicide Is Painless," which I had taught myself on the recorder, or, remaining within the confines of the den on the braided oval rug or at the child-sized Formica-and-chrome table, which was about a quarter the size of the TV set, busy myself with a coloring book—I would be glad to watch whatever they were watching. Not only was there no V-chip in the free love era, but—other than the progressive academics advocating for Children's Television Workshop—there was little in the way of caring about the effect of TV-watching on kids. My parents were devotees of the Movie of the Week, which was a crap shoot by nature, and they readily gave in to serendipity and inertia. I once asked my mother about the plot of one of these as I weighed my activity options, and she said, "It's about a monster who rapes women." I heard "a monster who rakes women" and saw, in my mind's eye, an actual monster (fashioned after some Saturday-afternoon movie—green, slimy, spiky, prominently fanged) wildly brandishing a yard rake with which he was terrorizing women all over town, leading to Tippi Hedren–esque screaming and flailing. I opted for my wind instrument.

This squandered teachable moment goes into the category of other misperceived explanations, such as the previously mentioned drug pushing and Mom's story about the "butcher" who pierced her ears, wherein I imagined my teenaged mom sitting in a barber chair beside a refrigerated glass case of pork shoulders as a man in a bloody white smock bent over her with a drill. There was also the time I asked her what the copyright symbol meant. Her accurate but extremely unhelpful response laden with a precariously unspecified indirect object was, "It means you can't copy it." I could not fathom why it was illegal and was sure such an honor system-based law was totally unenforceable. But just to prove it, I doodled the thing all over my drawing pad waiting excitedly for the FBI (which I knew all about from the TV series starring the dashing Efram Zimbalist Jr., and which I inexplicably referred to as *The BBI*) to come knocking. In a related subfile is my long-held belief that my parents wrote the Beatles song "Do You Want to Know a Secret?" because they were singing it once and I asked them if they made it up and they said yes. I found out the truth in a humiliating way when I announced this factoid to a friend (and her more knowledgeable parent) when the song came on the car radio.

Speaking of cars, on long rides during summer vacation—upstate New York to Washington, DC, Cape Cod, Bar Harbor, even Toronto took longer than you would think—I reveled in my temporary home in the backseat of our Cutlass Supreme that was jarringly and unnecessarily furnished with CB radio (more cumbersome antennae). This designated area was outfitted to approximate a portable replica of my bedroom, replete with Holly Hobbie quilt and pillow set and stuffed animals (at least one trip included an entire Samoyed family: dad, mom, and baby Velcroed to mom's underside) and well-stocked with books and word search puzzles. It was several years pre-Walkman, and apart from *Free to Be . . . You and Me*, my desert-island album that I wax on about in the next chapter, I didn't miss music when I left home. But I did pine for TV. When my mother tired of playing the license plate game and I Spy, I was forced to daydream, where I conjured up a *Jetsons*-like fantastical invention of a mini-TV that I could hold in my hand and watch any of the four channels I wanted. I didn't think, "There are transistor radios, why can't someone make transistor TVs?" or "Someday. . . ." I thought I was a crazy fantasizer, and again in my egocentric innocence, the only one to come up with such an idea. A generation later, kids in backseats on the New York State Thruway and the Massachusetts Turnpike are unaware of anything outside the car (or inside their own heads), because *Dora the Explorer* is on their own handheld iPad mini.

At some point in the 1980s or 1990s, it became a shameful thing to let TV babysit your kids. If this string of self-indulgent reminiscences does nothing else, it should demonstrate that we were in good hands—at least most of the time. TV may have offered us a sip of her beer and had her boyfriend over, but she knew we could handle it. Some of us pulled and smushed it like so much Silly Putty into a lifelong pursuit. I'll turn back to my early exposure musings as well as to Ken Jennings and *Planet Funny*. Jennings told actor/comedian Joel Hodgson about his thirteen-year-old son's love of *Mystery Science Theatre 3000* (created by Hodgson), despite its being a retro show from the previous century. Hodgson's response explains a lot to me. He was not surprised by the kid's enthusiasm for something from his dad's era. "Kids like the show," Hodgson told Jennings, "and they don't have a problem with references they don't understand, because their life is like that. They're constantly being confronted with things they don't understand, but they start to find meaning in the words and the tone in which they're delivered. The way we move into the world is the same way. You kind of learn things by proxy." So the family-values Cassandras had reason to fear the effects of wicked TV, and I had reason to attribute my personality development to it as well.

The cross section of 1965 viewing options I described earlier is the stuff now used in classrooms. It's archival. I am archival. *The James Beard Show* and *The Dr. Joyce Brothers Show*, both of which were created in the mid-1960s, like me, and both of which I grew up to write about decades later, are considered part of my penchant for "television history." Whereas to you it is plain as day that my interest in TV is really an excuse to revisit the events of my own life and the attending cultural events, it took me many years to realize this. I thought that I had honestly latched onto a subject of scholarly interest that befit my intellectual curiosity and capacity, but I confess that I am not much of a historian. I start to lose interest in a subject that happened too long before I was born. I started reading

Kurt Andersen's *Fantasyland: How America Went Haywire: A 500-Year History* several hundred pages in, when he gets to the 1960s and, not incidentally, where he begins talking about mass media and entertainment (I'm sure you'll find his treatment of the previous 450 years just as compelling as I found the last 50, if you are more open-minded and curious than I am, or if you are just as self-indulgent but hundreds of years older than me). This is why the real selling point of TV history as an ideal subject for me is the bite-sized brevity of the medium's history. But I have ceased judging myself by this measure. You may continue to judge me in this way, as long as you don't tell me so. The personal doesn't diminish the intellectual. Allow me to twist the slogan of my second-wave sisters and declare that the personal is the intellectual. Just look at all the computer geeks and filmmakers who made hay of their childhood passions. Obliquely comparing myself to Steven Spielberg and Gloria Steinem seems like a good way to end this chapter.

3

Love Letters

My love of television grew as I did and expanded to include all manner of sitcoms, variety shows, and dramas. I was really no different from my peers in the avid consumption. But I added a private component that signaled the beginning of an earnest endeavor. I can only assume that it began with my certifiable obsession with the *Free to Be . . . You and Me* album that was released in 1972 and was posthaste introduced to my second-grade class by our teacher, Miss Levy. She got married during the holiday break and took her husband's last name and became Ms. Mintz (baby steps). If I am certain of one explanation in my life, it is that the combination of Ms. Mintz, Marlo Thomas, Harry Belafonte, Alan Alda, Rosey Grier, Dudley Pippin, Atalanta, and Mel Brooks singing and storytelling about how boys can cry and play with dolls, and girls can grow up to be doctors (and/or welders, taxi drivers, poetry makers) and choose not to be wives is the stuff from which I am made.

It wasn't like an awakening. I was a seven-year-old girl, not a hampered housewife whose creative dreams had been quashed by domestic burdens and the patriarchy. The concepts of gender inequality and self-esteem had not yet presented as tangible problems in my brief existence. But the music was addictive and the spoken word pieces so rhythmic and begging to be memorized that I absorbed every bit of *Free to Be* effortlessly and ecstatically. I listened to the record constantly on my turntable that closed up into a plastic white suitcase with an orange handle. I listened to it for years, never tiring of it or the fuchsia album cover or of the booklet it came with or the separate *Free to Be . . . You and Me* book with a plethora of visually diverse bonus material and musical scores. The latter came in handy when I accompanied myself and a classmate on the piano as we sang "When We Grow Up" at a coffeehouse night in *college*. Whither the chutzpah?

After about three years of wearing down those LP grooves and perfecting my impression of Billy De Wolfe's recitation of "Don't Dress Your Cat in an Apron," a tragedy occurred, the horror of which I can relive forty years later. My record player was situated on a shelf above which and to the right were several books, reined in by the head-and-torso half of a brass dachshund. For no apparent reason other than God hating me, while I sat on my bed listening and fetishizing over the *FTB . . . YAM* accompanying documents, the fore-dachshund fell onto the record while it was playing and cleaved it clean in half. The ensuing events are blurred into one, wherein I flew screaming and crying to wherever my parents were—surely they thought I had accidently stabbed myself in the eye with a compass—and the next thing I knew (it might have not been the same day, but I have to believe they couldn't tolerate me otherwise), we were at the Big N variety store buying a replacement. By then it was the reissue version produced by Arista, not the original Bell, but by some miracle that detail went blessedly unnoticed by me.

Thanks to the earlier work of Marlo Thomas—aka Ann Marie, aka *That Girl*—I was already inculcated by her agenda.

By kindergarten, I understood organically that women could live on their own and make their way in the world and that department-store-window mannequins were sometimes live people. I already loved Marlo, and it must have been all I talked about throughout early elementary school, so much so that my mother perhaps suggested, not quite but almost with the tone of "why don't you marry her?" that I write her a letter. To this day, I have no recollection, nor does my mother, of how we knew where to send such a thing, but my mother must have had the recessive gene of the librarian that I became, because over the next several years, she managed to provide me with effective addresses for (all three of) the TV networks.

The first communiqué, naturally, was to Marlo. I have no record of what I wrote to her, but one can imagine the sincere handwriting and brusque tone of a child's correspondence—"Dear Ms. Thomas, I like your show *That Girl* and the *Free to Be . . . You and Me* record. You are my favorite. Please send me a picture of you. Sincerely, Kathleen Collins." Something of that nature. I hit the jackpot on my first go-round. Marlo had a fan club, and its president shipped me a full-on portfolio of glossy promotional photos of Marlo in different poses, one gorgeously signed, "With warm wishes, Marlo," along with a letter on pink paper in fancy typed script. It also came with a fan club membership card and was all enclosed in an appropriate fuchsia folder with a thick slab of cardboard for protection during its journey. My parents, who normally did not abide clutter, allowed me to exhibit the signed letter on the refrigerator door.

With the unexpected and welcome success of my correspondence with her, Marlo was my gateway to a chain of my TV heroes over the next few years, otherwise known by anyone with eyes or ears, and as previously stated, as the golden age of television. I occasionally strayed from TV proper—Valerie Harper,

Julie Kavner, Mary Tyler Moore, Carol Burnett, Sally Struthers, Suzanne Pleshette, Michael Learned, Melissa Gilbert, the lone (John) boy, Richard Thomas—and into recording artist territory with Barbra Streisand, Helen Reddy, Olivia Newton John, Sonny & Cher, and Tony Orlando & Dawn. I don't recall ever being rebuffed, though I have to wonder why Carly Simon is not represented, given that I knew every track of *No Secrets* and *Hotcakes* by heart. As my special pastime roughly coincided with a pen pal project in fourth grade where we of the Brighton school district were paired with similarly aged counterparts in Brighton, England, I must have applied my new genteel skills to the extra-credit level by prevailing upon TV stars. If I could write to nine-year-old Leslie in the UK, why not nine-year-old Kami Cotler, who probably had school in a trailer between shooting scenes for *The Waltons*? The only difference I could see was that to correspond with Leslie I needed to use the exotic feathery blue airmail paper that folded into an envelope.

While most responses from the TV stars were the standard-issue typed generic letter ("Dear Friend, It means so much to me to know that you enjoy our show as much as we enjoy doing it . . . Thank you for taking the time to write to me. Best wishes . . .") accompanied by a 3 x 5 or glossy 8 x 10 photo that nonetheless thrilled me with each postal delivery, there were occasional outliers. Melissa Sue Anderson, *Little House on the Prairie*'s Mary, sent a single-spaced typed letter filling up 1.5 pages with packaged descriptions of her leisure time activities, how much she admires her TV parents, Michael Landon and Karen Grassle, and how she'd like to be an actress when she grows up, but "only time will tell." Kami Cotler's letters were brief but *handwritten* on the blank sides of actual script pages. When I looked at them a few years later, it dawned on me that the handwriting was suspiciously neat, even and adultish. If someone researching my papers after my death were to find this stash and not know about the classroom pen pal training, it would seem that I had the makings of a celebrity stalker:

> Dear Kathleen, Thank you for writing to me again. I'm happy that you like the idea of being just 3 days older than me. Keep watching, Kami Cotler
>
> Dear Kathleen, Thank you for writing to me again, and for the birthday wishes. I hope you had a good time camping on your birthday. Keep watching, Kami Cotler.
>
> Dear Kathleen, Thanks for writing to me again. I get a lot of fan mail, and it's very hard to find the time to answer it, so it's very hard to be a pen-pal with everyone. Keep watching, Kami Cotler.

Another thanked me for the Christmas card. In my hypothetical posthumous defense, however, Kami or her proxy made the mistakes of a) revealing too much personal info in her first missive with "I'm 9 years old and will be 10 on June 17th," and b) egging me on.

Amidst my robust success, there was an unfortunate incident related to *Little House on the Prairie*, which, given an investigation of the postmark on the envelope, might indicate the end of my activities in this area. Karen Grassle, "Ma Ingalls," had a fan club, though it was nowhere near the professional caliber of Marlo's. The president was probably a tween, her address revealing that she lived in Winchester, Illinois, and the newsletter was a stapled assortment of mimeographed pages. Nevertheless, inspired by the postcard photo I had received from an earlier fan club mailing of the entire Ingalls family, I decided to render them in illustrated form and submit it to the newsletter for publication. While I possessed no stunning artistic ability, I could draw neatly and create recognizable personages, especially when provided with salient props like suspenders and bonnets—the sort of drawing a developmental psychologist would evaluate as flowing from the crayon of a non-troubled if middling child. The president/editor accepted my submission, but the drawing I had done—in recently sharpened crayons and executed with obvious effort and thought—had turned into a messy line drawing that looked like the scrawls of a nascent sociopath. The only reason I knew it was "mine" was that the credit line (not in my handwriting) read, "Kathleen Collins, Rochester, NY." I couldn't have known better, at that innocent age (I was also clearly ignorant of the fact that my colorful drawing could not be replicated in a mimeograph), not to get involved with such an obviously corrupt, morally bereft celebrity tabloid. Live and learn. This event may well be the source of my violent reaction to the monstrous and aesthetically mangled solicitations of predatory academic journals.

This was a private pursuit. It wasn't that I intentionally kept my activities a secret; I just never felt a strong desire to share it with anyone. Nor did I go to school telling everyone I played solo games of Yahtzee twelve times in a row or opened up a "shop" in my closet where I sold homemade wares to my parents and stuffed animals. It was extracurricular. Though the fruits of my proto celebrity stalking would have been the ideal fodder for show-and-tell, I am sure I felt the material evidence was too valuable to ferry to school—and this is where my only-childness if not prissy character does present itself—where my fellow second-graders' sticky hands would destroy them. There was no open trading market like that available to baseball card or today's Pokémon aficionados. There may have been an underground community, but if so, I was not aware of it, and how could I ever have learned about it? I didn't need to show off about it. The communication and accumulation was satisfying in and of itself.

Whether I stopped sending fan letters because I was embittered or whether I grew out of it, I'm not sure. But I know that the letters and photos have been important enough to carry around with me all the decades since, rather than toss them or leave them to get lost or "in there somewhere" with my other childhood belongings in my parents' storage warrens. I did add to the collection once as a teen—it was Timothy Hutton, albeit a movie star, whose people sent a postcard photo of him in a tweed newsboy cap, though this one has mysteriously disappeared—and twice as an adult, when I felt excited enough by a TV personality. I still have no recollection of what I wrote at the age of thirty, but I am certain I tried to be charming enough to encourage a personal response or invitation to appear on their shows. The first of this limited series was to David Letterman just after the move to CBS, and the other was to Rosie O'Donnell after the premiere of her daytime talk show in 1996. Representatives for both responded, but neither one included a letter, only a glossy 8 x 10.

If I were to draw a conclusion from this small sample size, I would have to say that the internet (making contact info available to a lab rat) is wonderful and horrible. In her 2018 book *Fame: The Hijacking of Reality*, Justine Bateman shares her perspective as the recipient of letters like mine (though I was totally devoted to *Family Ties*, Justine, M. J. Fox and Meredith Baxter Birney—whom I already admired from the evanescent 1972 sitcom *Bridget Loves Bernie*, about an interfaith marriage, and a bit later *Family*, where she played Quinn Cummings's adoptive older sister—the show ran far outside the margins of my hobby).

She appreciates what it took to address a celebrity in the 1980s and 1990s and how the rigmarole attests to the dedication of the fan, which is not the case today. I'd like to think I was special, as Mister Rogers impressed upon me, and I appreciate Justine's generous stance, but it was really the only option.

I am still star-struck to some degree, though I hate the term, and have channeled a simmering obsession into writing about the concept of celebrity from an aloof academic position. I now recognize that celebrities are real people and often not worthy of such lionization. But I still get a thrill when I see them walking around (Jimmy Fallon, Kevin Nealon), eating in the same no-frills restaurant as me (David Hyde Pierce, Uma Thurman), or standing in a checkout line at a Dean & Deluca (Dame Maggie Smith). It's sure to be an obvious statement, but I email and @ famouspeople *a lot*. Wonderful and horrible.

At NYU's graduate journalism program, my advisor was Ellen Willis, the cultural critic who wrote about rock music, politics, feminism, and lots of other important things in an incisive, satisfyingly persuasive style. If there is a patron saint of my persistence in television studies, it is Ellen, but more on that later. Ellen and I went to dinner one night at Minetta Tavern on MacDougal Street in the West Village, and afterward we repaired to my fifth-floor walkup on West Third Street (I had moved on up from Brooklyn). Readers of a certain cultural stripe may be wowed by this celebrity connection about which I seem to be humblebragging, and they would be completely justified, though I was a bit too square to be wowed, and also she was such an unbelievably unassuming person that any jitters on my part came not from her cultural icon status but from her role as my professor. I'm sure the reason we got to the point of her coming over was that I was doing most of the chattering all night (her rousing writing belied her agonizingly quiet live-person demeanor) and probably told her about my TV fan letter collection. So I invited her up to see my proverbial etchings, and because she was kind and really seemed to care about her students, she accepted. I remember fanning them out proudly, really for the first time to anyone in years, on the only horizontal surface in my apartment other than the floor as she took them in, in her serious, quiet way. "You should write about these," she said. Finally, Ellen (she died in 2006), I am.

4

Little Women

Despite my feminist training from Ms. Mintz and Marlo Thomas and some TV characters I will address in a moment, I was still a girl growing up in 1970s America. I had Barbie and several Barbie properties—camper, townhouse and private plane. "How," I never wondered, "did Barbie get so rich?" The lack of business attire, rich husband, or ex, and the fact that she was almost always clad in only a sky blue one-piece bathing suit and doing a bunch of nothing did not give me pause. Her anatomically indicting figure was mitigated only slightly by the constant presence of her flat-chested, flat-footed kid sister, Skipper.

Angie and Dawn were smaller fashion dolls—six inches to Barbie's nearly twelve—who were more obsessed with clothes. Their feet conveniently had holes in the bottom, so they could be impaled on pegs attached to their battery-powered runway track, down which they jerkily sashayed. Dusty, the rather butch golf champion (certainly in juxtaposition to the uber-feminine Barbie), lent gravitas to the group, because she had solid skills and a profession. She was the same height as Barbie, but because she had the flat feet of an athlete and not the permanently shortened calf muscles of a stiletto-wearing lay-about sun goddess, she seemed stockier. She, too, had holes in her feet to secure her to the putting green when she swung, which I thought was wholly unnecessary. It goes without saying that every lady facsimile mentioned here had the smooth and shiny hair fit for a Pantene commercial.

All of these dolls did their job of inserting the proper female beauty standard into my young, impressionable brain, but that message really took hold with vise-grip power thanks to three annual televised beauty pageants. I never understood the difference between the Miss America and Miss USA—you might think that Miss America, the classic one with the famous song, hosted by Bert Parks, included all of the Americas, but it was 1973, and it was a beauty pageant, so . . . no. Miss Universe, hosted by Bob Barker, was my favorite, because it seemed exciting with all those visitors from around the world, but I eagerly anticipated each one. My friend Amy and I had a special ritual wherein we prepared Buitoni canned ravioli and pulled out the convertible red Naugahyde couch in my den for the fullest judging comfort. We focused intensely on all aspects of the competition and chose the "prettiest" winners. We forgot everything by the next day (never knew the winner's name to begin with, only the state she represented) and didn't follow through to see if Miss America kept her promises. But we spent the rest of our lives trying to unlearn every idea we nonetheless absorbed from watching these events. I could say much more about the implications of female foot mutilation and sexual objectification, but it's time to go peel off my Crest White Strips.

These competition events bring to mind the Olympics. Now that's a television event that used to matter. I didn't care about the USA, medals won, or team sports. Not surprisingly, I homed in on skating and gymnastics. Amy and I tittered about the "profiles" of the male gymnasts, in disbelief that we were allowed to look at people's barely covered private parts for that long without getting in trouble. I idolized Olga Korbut, Nadia Comenici, and Tai Babilonia. I refused to accept the fact that I did not have a gymnast's strength, flexibility, or fearlessness. I took part in intramural gymnastics, which was basically after-school remedial sports for the unfit and unskilled. My friend Buffy was the type who could do a standing back flip on the sidewalk in front of her house in her street clothes without even a warm-up toe-touch, whereas I could do half-decent front and back walkovers after warming up for two to three hours. For years, I prepared to execute a back handspring, crouching, in position, but never springing. I believed I could eventually do a split (the front kind, as the Chinese kind were completely out of the question) if I pushed a little further every day, which I would do while watching TV. No one ever explained to me that not all bodies work the same. I watched the Olympic gymnasts barely touch the floor in their routines and fly across the balance beam as if they had the weight of a bird. Similarly with ice-skating, in real life, my ankles became tired and crampy as soon as I tied the laces.

In non-Olympic years during high school, we were sated by Deney Terrio's *Dance Fever*, the precursor to *Dancing with the Stars*, but instead of C-list and D-list celebrity *contestants* who could actually dance, it featured the 1980 post-prime celebrity counterparts as *judges* who could not. The fever was contagious in this realm, too, and my friends and I, lacking any ability in choreography or dancing or lifting people, as well as that Napoleon Dynamite passion, would start out at a high pitch but lose our mojo after about five minutes. On my own time, I would also vicariously join the *Soul Train* and *American*

Bandstand dance parties, moving to the groove and getting the funk, much as I do now when any Bee Gees or Kool & the Gang song comes up on the playlist and no one's watching.

The Olympics coverage provided plot and drama in the sports themselves, the proverbial thrill of victory and agony of defeat. For those of us that weren't so keen on certain sports, the networks made sure we were provided with the plot and drama of the athletes' backstories. But I fell out by the time Mary Lou Retton got her Wheaties box, heard only snippets of Bob Costas's sentimental side dishes, and knew of Picabo Street only because of her singular name and would not have been able to recall her excellence in alpine ski racing without Wikipedia, though I did know it was something snow-related. I was lured back in a limited and brief way when Dave Letterman sent his mother to cover the 1992 summer games in Barcelona. That marked the end of the more spectacular, anticipatory quadrennial event, and I have to think that for most of America, the Olympics, thenceforth taking place biennially—compounded by the ease of on-demand, time-shifted, computer-assisted viewing—have lost a substantial share of its propagandizing and aspirational power. In 1994 I was sucked into the Nancy-Tonya vortex, but I'll get to that later.

After explaining earlier that I preferred shows based in reality, it will sound like a contradiction to say that *I Dream of Jeannie* was one of my staples. I wanted to be Jeannie so much that I would deliberately daydream about it. I had no interest in being a servant and/or wife of an astronaut—what I coveted were her digs and her powers. I wanted to live in Jeannie's bottle more than anything. The idea of being surrounded by all those brightly colored fabrics and pillows was the epitome of luxury and coziness. And her magic abilities, unlike *Bewitched*'s

Samantha's, were boundless. Sam had to go through laborious incantations to make things happen, and her powers were vulnerable to a host of nefarious obstacles—a bitter relative, her own pregnancy, exotic illness, etc. (also, I could not twitch my nose and had to resort to baby Tabitha's manual method, which I feel certain was added by the writers for the very purpose of pacifying vulnerable viewers like me). Jeannie merely had to cross her arms and blink her eyes and Bob's your uncle. Like Samantha, however, she had an uptight and controlling man (at least with Original Darrin) whose potential wrath kept each from fully using her gifts.

It's painfully obvious what was going on here. Media scholar Susan J. Douglas described it perfectly:

> You could almost see these guys holding their nuts for dear life. Sensing they were playing with fire, they tried to contain it technologically, through images of levitation, twitching noses, and poofs of fake smoke. . . . Whenever women used these powers outside the home, in the public sphere, the male world was turned completely upside down. Business simply could not be conducted as usual, and logic and rationality were often overthrown and rendered useless. Men were made impotent by these powers . . . and were stripped of their male authority and made to look foolish and incompetent in front of their male superiors.

Their double-edge identities, mysterious, all-powerful, uncontrollable witch and genie, were problematic in normal everyday society, and/but they made for great television. The programs originally aired in prime time, so the marital strife was even more relevant and titillating. And speaking of marital strife, Lucille Ball was a member of this club, too. She didn't have supernatural powers, but she was magical, and her vivacious, quirky charm was a perceived threat to her husband's babalu career. I loved Lucy and all her iterations, from the black-and-white apartment dwelling one, to the one whose intro featured a Lucy puppet in top hat, bare legs, and tails, though I merge the plots and characters, reliably placing Gale Gordon's boss characters Mr. Mooney and Mr. Carter in the wrong sitcoms. There's another flaxen-haired maiden to add to the bunch, too. I quoted this same Susan Douglas passage, from *Where the Girls Are: Growing Up Female with Mass Media*, in my book about Dr. Joyce Brothers where I compare her TV presence to that of Jeannie and Samantha: "Joyce did not have magical powers, but she did have knowledge and intellect, uncommon (at least in their public expression on television) and intimidating traits and mysterious skills in a woman during the 1950s and 60s."

I was, at the time, unaware that my frustration was the result of the baked-in sexism in the plots of these shows. "Come on, Ricky, just let her be in the show!" "Why does Jeannie have to stay home instead of going to the banquet with you?" Darrin wouldn't let Sam use her powers to make her life easier, even though she was often pressed to make dinner at the last minute for Larry Tate and clients. On the final episode of *Mad Men*, set in 1970, Joan broke free from her beau because he didn't want her to fulfill her entrepreneurial dream (at which she was already proving successful). There are countless examples of women being stifled or bottled or zipped up right on up until *Girls*' Shoshanna, whose self-interested Jason Ritter boyfriend (nearly) squelches her ambitions. They are couched in entertainment and often in comedy, so we laugh and cluck our tongues at the same time. But enough of these scenarios aggregating over enough years might explain why, when I entered my twenties and was enjoined by a random man on the street to smile, I would have given my nose-twitching left arm to have magical powers.

I watched *Bewitched* and *I Dream of Jeannie* mostly in syndication and was at the mercy of whatever episode was aired. It if was a rerun, I watched it. If I missed an episode, I suffered. I had a habit of scrutinizing the TV listings in the newspaper—the much-pored-over standalone TV section that came with the Sunday paper was more compelling to me than the comics—and trying to figure out how I could access the out-of-market channels that were cruelly listed along with the local stations. I could eke out grainy images on those mysterious out-of-town stations (a silver lining of not flipping too fast), and I discovered by accident that if I held the channel dial at just the right position between numbers, I could improve the image a bit. It would be worth it for me to hold it there in an unnatural position for several minutes, fancying myself a modern-day Thomas Edison, inhabiting the essence of television itself—far-seeing. Now *that* was fine tuning. The only other experience that allowed me that thrill of imagining myself able to see things that many other people couldn't see were not psychotic fugue states but rather my visits to the UCLA Film & Television Archive. Though that activity borders on sounding elitist—lah-di-dah! look at you flying across the country to see rare clips of the unproduced pilot of *Saucepans and the Single Girl* starring Barbara Feldon that is not available to us mortals!—it might have been in practice but not in spirit.

Based on what I watched most often, I exhibited a penchant for laugh tracks, a diverse color palette, and funny, if oppressed, ladies. Things got noticeably better for the latter in the 1970s, mostly thanks to Norman Lear and MTM Enterprises. Where the sexism went over my head (but straight into my soul) with their predecessors, I could tell that the seventies' brigade of relatively liberated women was cut of a different cloth. And because they fit into my *Free to Be* paradigm, I recognized and appreciated it. There were women making it on their own, either by choice or by circumstances, with and without children—Mary Richards, Rhoda Morgenstern, Ann Romano, Florida Evans after James's death, Alice Hyatt—or comfortably independent of their spouses (unlike Samantha and Jeannie), either because they had a strong enough marriage—Maude, Gloria Stivic—or because they were good at ignoring or defying their spouses—Phyllis Lindstrom before and after Lars's death, and only occasionally but therefore all the more powerfully, Edith Bunker. In my rough draft of this book, it was right here that I had a note that read: "research re women's movement effect on TV shows and vice versa." There are loads of such research by scholars and journalists that you can find yourself or ask your librarian, but those encapsulations "do not belong to this memoir" as Marge Piercy wrote in hers, *Sleeping with Cats* (though she was referring to two of her mother's marriages). I am doing everything in my power not to share several citations, including , L. C. Spangler, *Television Women from Lucy to Friends: Fifty Years of Sitcoms and Feminism* (Praeger, 2003); L. Rabinovitz, "Sitcoms and Single Moms: Representations of Feminism on American TV" in *Cinema Journal* 29 (1989); and the aforementioned Susan Douglas book.

The televised lives of women and girls were of supreme interest to me. It was not as if I was seeking them out, but I was naturally and magnetically drawn to their behavior, appearance, antics, plight, anxieties, and rewards. In a word, they were role models, for better or worse. *Crazy Ex-Girlfriend*'s star and cocreator, Rachel Bloom, has admitted that her title character, Rebecca Bunch—whose antics, plight, and anxieties make Lucille Ball seem like Ruth Bader Ginsburg—may not be the greatest role model, but it's an honest portrayal of a modern woman living with real-life problems (in a show that's as fun and addictive to watch as a mash-up of *Melrose Place*, *Glee*, and *Pee-wee's Playhouse*). This raises a question: What serves women best? Aspirational, lean-in stories or naked bulbs revealing bare faces and tummy rolls? Now that there is room for all permutations, there is no real need to answer the question, but if pushed to choose, I prefer the Rachel Bloom approach. That might be my age, or it might be the age we are in, but one can only take so much unattainable lifestyle purveyance. Let's remember that it's not in TV's job description to serve women anyway, so when we get something good and true, it's worth singing about.

All the role models, the good, the bad and the pretty-ugly have always been counted among my friends, no less so than how Michelle Obama and Cher are my friends because I follow them on Twitter. Actually, a *little* less so, since Eve Plumb recently liked one of my Tweets, and with the exception of Mister Rogers and *Romper Room*'s Miss Rita (she could *see* me! or so I chose to believe when she alit on "Kathy," which is also the closest I could ever come to my name on a personalized leather bracelet), no one on my TV ever gave me the time of day. I should have taken courage from some of my girls on TV, but instead I just got good at noting how different we sometimes were.

Laura Ingalls was a virtual mentor in many ways, but I could never have stood up to Nellie Oleson the way she did. I discovered my instinctive desire to tame and charm mean girls from Laura's relationship with her prairie frenemy Nellie. Laura was an admirable foil to Nellie's entitled, ringleted snot, but I betrayed my wimpy colors as I silently begged Laura to relent and comply—just play Ring Around the Rosie like Nellie wants! Everything will be so much easier! If I attended their one-room schoolhouse, I would have tried to be Nellie's friend above all else, even if it meant sacrificing my authentic self. (I felt the same way about placating Cordelia in Margaret Atwood's *Cat's Eye*, painfully identifying with Elaine.) I was never really bullied, but I harbored a dire fear of being the outcast or not being liked by absolutely everyone. At the very least I wished to go along completely unnoticed. There was one girl in elementary school who told me she was the boss of me and wouldn't let me go home as we passed my own driveway, and another in middle school who seemed to resent me for being sibling-free, the only person to viciously call me a "spoiled brat." She had double initials, but I never wished her to be kidnapped and murdered—I just wanted her to like me. I wonder if she possessed that bad-seed trait of preying on the weak and could sniff out my fundamental truth, that as an only child I lacked the sparring skills to defend myself against the Nellies, the Cordelias, and her own girl gang leader ilk. I am aware that Nellie and Laura became actual friends as adults, but I had stopped watching by then, and the self-realization was locked in. I still reflexively rely on kindness as self-defense despite the damage to my internal organs.

My real-life girlfriend relationships rarely looked like the ones I saw on TV. My close friends and I didn't link arms or lie all over each other like Lena Dunham and her *Girls* squad. We didn't cry and fight ferociously. Was I missing out on life's true satisfactions? Were my relationships hollow? Was I choosing the wrong friends? Was it me? Did it occur to me that those representations were someone's fantasy? Isn't most of TV? Isn't that its main purpose? My life was more like that of *Square Pegs*' Lauren and Patty, an insecure duo wishing for popularity and forming an intimate bond in never fully achieving it. Naturally, that more realistic portrayal lasted only one season, though as it was my senior year of high school, it came along at exactly the right moment. When Sarah Jessica Parker came back, however, she had blossomed into Carrie Bradshaw.

I was apprehensive about *Sex and the City* at the outset. The apparent focus on manic dating and fashion, notably footwear, signaled that it was not a show for me. I avoided it without much difficulty, given that I didn't subscribe to HBO, and there was a lot of other important work to be done in the late 1990s that I'll get to in a later chapter. There was little acceptable reason—my friends and a voice inside chided me—for my not watching it pointedly, if not appointmently. It was with some trifling irritation that I recognized the characters were generally my age (SJP herself born in the same year), living in the city where I was living and featured a journalist (I had just graduated from journalism school and was still hoping to become a cultural critic). I also missed *Freaks and Geeks,* which aired on network TV the following year and which represented my very cohort at an earlier age and had a cult following and was clearly meant for me, but I was neither aware of nor felt any chafing about it. Sometimes, too, you just can't know how important something is until years later, after it's been culturally metabolized. And the cusp of the millennium was wasted on obsessive commotion about Y2K and internet startups instead of recognizing the signs that we were inching toward a colossal golden age of TV that would have a more significant and lasting impact on the nation that either of those flashes-in-the-pan.

When *Sex and the City*'s regrettably censored TBS syndication began what seemed like mere minutes after the HBO run ended, I admitted I'd been lying to myself about my desire to watch it, and I made amends. So let's get right to everyone's first question. Though I should have wanted to be a Carrie, owing to her glamorous career, there was no getting around my

Mirandaness. Miranda, like me, would have totally preferred Danny Partridge over Keith, and nebbishy, smartass *Northern Exposure* doc Joel Fleischman over heartthrob DJ Chris (who, not at all incidentally, showed up as Carrie's nicest hottie boyfriend, Aidan). Beyond the unabashed pleasure the show delivered, it has, in the intervening years, become a cultural hallmark as iconic as *The Sopranos. SATC* is trotted out on a regular basis as a comparison to any ensemble or group buddy vehicle (*Girls, Entourage, The L Word*, even *Call the Midwife*), and the four archetypes continue to be employed. The *New Yorker*'s Emily Nussbaum used the occasion of the publication of Brett Martin's *Difficult Men: Behind the Scenes of a Creative Revolution from "The Sopranos" and "The Wire" to "Mad Men"* to reminisce about *Sex and the City*, nine years after the show's end and five years shy of being able to peg it to Miranda's, er, Cynthia Nixon's run for New York governor and the show's twentieth anniversary. In her article titled "Difficult Women," she forced readers to revisit the show, take it out of its stylish pink box and appreciate the complexity of the characters as more than just one-dimensional checkboxes on a BuzzFeed quiz. In an essay I wrote about *Absolutely Fabulous*'s Eddie and Patsy wherein I admitted to preferring the less-realistic portrayal of their friendship and dysfunction to that of *SATC* with its escapist properties, I nevertheless identified what I saw as *SATC*'s social value: "Couched in a highly palatable fantasy, the show brought our real-life issues to television. We hoped our mothers and boyfriends would watch so they could hear incisive Carrie explain what the trouble was, so we could say, 'See? It's not just me!'"

TV is one of those places, as in music, where we act cool and pretend to superficially enjoy a show for its pop entertainment value but are too proud to admit that it really digs a deeper groove in our psyche. *SATC* is one of those shows. I remember feeling vindicated upon reading Nussbaum's treatise, even though I didn't think anything had been bothering me before. In her memoir *My Brilliant Friends: Our Lives in Feminism*, Nancy Miller writes, "There's nothing like death to offer the kind of closure that allows for shapely storytelling." Miller is referring to elegies for friends, but this beautifully succinct thought can apply to any event that has been completed and can be talked about in comprehensive and comprehensible ways only when it has a clear end. Then it can live on indefinitely in the things we say about it and in how we decide what it means to us—and, per usual, I mean that in the first-person plural as well as the cultural "us." The fact that *SATC* was a compelling subject of anniversary journalism in 2018 is a hint that the show will probably be kicking around in our heads until the last thoughts fall out.

5

King Lear and Queen Mary

I have great respect for people like Joan Ganz Cooney and Lloyd Morrisett, cofounders of the Children's Television Workshop, as well all the other developmental psychologists and producers (and hippie, guitar-playing teachers) who cared about young brains and building character and citizenship delivered in a colorful candy-coated shell. And I benefited from their work. I learned about cooperation, racial and ability differences, self-expression, self-esteem, and kindness from their shows without realizing it. But other programs, the ones that were targeting not me but my elders, were educational, too. While *Sesame Street* and other public broadcasting productions satisfied the Reithian trinity of information, education, and entertainment in the spirit in which it was intended, *All in the Family* did so perhaps inadvertently. While I still struggle with being able to articulate the difference between information and education (if you know something, then you've learned it and therefore have been educated—am

I wrong?), it's the line between education and entertainment that has served as my biding interest all these years. In many cases, the line is about a pixel wide. I use the Trojan Horse analogy often when referring to this trinity—which, let's be honest, the British Broadcasting Corporation also plays fast and loose with even without the mercenary determinants of ratings and advertising dollars—thereby illustrating that I remember some things from high school English. Education by covert means is how TV must operate, especially for children and lazy people. And also, what constitutes education? What subject matter is being taught? How a bill becomes a law, sure. But also how there are people in the world who don't trust or respect other people based on skin color or how what the man says carries the day. How can I become a fully aware adult if someone doesn't teach or indirectly show me these painful facts at an early age?

Whereas my educational TV viewing took place chez Grandma Deedle on the goldenrod-carpeted porch, the golden-age line-up—*All in the Family*, *The Mary Tyler Moore Show*, *The Bob Newhart Show*, and *The Carol Burnett Show*—was frequently screened in my grandparents' bedroom. I lay prone, chin in hands, at the foot of my grandfather's twin bed, a three-foot ocean between my eyes and the portable TV where it sat on its rolling cart. Grandma Deedle watched along with me, but in a more dignified fashion on her adjacent bed, propped against the headboard and several pillows and multitasking with the crossword. She was the age I am as I write this (which gives me enormous pause when I think about how much the world has changed since then but also about how I now multitask with the crossword puzzle while watching TV with numerous pillows supporting my back). That prime-time block was my favorite two hours of the week.

Much ink has been well spent on the brilliance and social impact of *All in the Family*. Of course there's no way of knowing what kind of person I would have been without this show—which I cross-list in the educational and entertainment categories—but it is hard to imagine that seeing such an array of people types and human issues in my formative years didn't give me at least a soupçon of empathy and open-mindedness. It also gave me the subject for two of my publications en route to tenure. I still watch it occasionally and believe it holds up (despite the insufferable acting of my closest stand-ins, Mike and Gloria). And as I write this, the show's legendary producer, Norman Lear, is in his mid-nineties and is as sharp as ever, lately hosting a podcast where he interviews the similarly admired TV creators and performers of the day, still skewering the racism, sexism, consumerism, and warmongering that fueled him in 1971 as it does in 2019. I watched almost every Norman Lear creation: *The Jeffersons*, *Maude*, *Good Times*, *Sanford and Son* (which I frequently confused with *Chico and the Man*, produced by James Komack, as they each featured a crotchety older man and a handsome younger man surrounded by uninteresting metal objects, and both had dissimilar but memorable theme songs), *Mary Hartman, Mary Hartman*, *One Day at a Time*. I still believe they are among the best shows that ever aired on TV.

Why I vividly though unspecifically recall a Lear series from 1975, *Hot L Baltimore*, or why I was even watching it in the first place, I cannot say. Obviously, at the age of ten, I wasn't reading TV criticism (where would one have done so, anyway?) and learning about new shows. I'd discover a program only if it appeared on the screen in front of me. Which was probably the case with *Hot L*, butting up against one of my staples. I was shocked to learn recently that it ran for only four months. I'm sure I had no idea Norman Lear created it or what it meant to be a Norman Lear production or who Normal Lear was, but I was likely attracted to it for the same reasons I was compelled to watch *All in the Family* (and *Soap*, two years after *Hot L* disappeared). My vague memory of it is largely a feeling that I was watching something decidedly not meant for me, because it featured prostitutes and gay people. But I was enchanted by the irreverence, a quality that, while I wasn't able to categorize it then, continues to be the most essential for me—in TV shows and in people.

Lear and his subjects were not the only critical players in the 1970s. On January 25, 2017, I received this via email from my friend Melinda: "Just saw the news that MTM has died. YOU were of course the first person I thought of. I have never been the kind of TV-watcher who could recite season and episode names and numbers, but the MTM Show def. had a big impact on my sense of what a woman could be. I refer to my years living on my own in Somerville as my Mary Tyler Moore years, and remember them with great fondness and wistfulness. Xoxo." Because I had foresworn social media and all news at this particular moment of US history, this was how I learned that Mary Tyler Moore had passed away, at age eighty. She was forever young, immortalized by her sweet, strong, and relatable single, professional-woman character.

It would be glib and revisionist to say that *The Bob Newhart Show* is the reason I have two degrees in psychology and wrote a book about a psychologist. But there's no evidence to prove it's not. Again, who knows what I'd be without that show? It is absolutely the reason that I revere Bob Newhart. And the best scenes were the ones that took place in his office. It might be notable, however, that I did not become a psychologist. Newhart is a national treasure, and while I could Chris Farley–fawn over him for some time, I'll just draw your attention to a couple of highlights from his later career. There must be at least a million of us who found Newhart's virtuoso "Stop it" treatment that appeared on a *MadTV* skit in 2001 to be the most cost- and psychologically effective therapy around. And the most mind-blowing, long-game TV crossover in history was the 1990 series finale of *Newhart*. If for some unfortunate reason you don't know what I'm referring to, I can't say anything more without spoiling it.

Just to make it clear for the younger readers, the 1970s were to comedy-variety shows what the 2010s are to podcasts. Everybody was doing it (but on only three outlets, not unlimited). *The Sonny and Cher Comedy Hour*, *Donny & Marie*, *The Hudson Brothers Razzle Dazzle Show*, *The Flip Wilson Show*, *The Captain and Tennille Show*, and *Tony Orlando & Dawn* were just the ones in my rotation. *The Carol Burnett Show*, however, was the most enduring and the winningest in every sense. I will refrain from listing everything that's so wonderful about Carol and the show. You already know about the *Gone with the Wind* parody, Mrs. Wiggins, and all the poignant-hilarious Eunice and Mama sketches. And how hunky Lyle Waggoner was, especially to a prepubescent girl who still thought (was socialized—by TV, that capricious devil!—to believe) debonair, James Bond types were the cat's pajamas.

I was perhaps as attached to *The Carol Burnett Show* as I was to my security blanket, Bee-do, who had disintegrated into so many pieces that my mother had no choice but to toss it, the (albeit appropriate) loss of which I am wincing about as I type. I lay in my hot bedroom one Saturday night after watching a season finale, circa 1972, whimpering self-indulgently but with genuine angst, until my mother obligingly came in to ask me what the matter was. I told her about the Carol Burnett–shaped hole in my life. I lingered on the image of her in her scullery maid's ensemble, on the dark stage in a single spotlight, singing something sad, tugging on her ear for what I believed to be the last time ever. My mother patiently, and most certainly stifling laughter, explained that it was only for the summer. Summer, the very idea of which normally induced breathless anticipation, took on a mournful cast. Pun intended. No Carol, no Harvey, no Tim, Vicki, or Lyle, no fabulous performances by Ray Charles, the Carpenters, the Pointer Sisters or Steve Lawrence and Eydie Gormé. I didn't understand the concept of summer hiatus and just felt bereft.

In 2017 I received an email from my mom, subject titled "TV alert," wherein she wanted me to know about the upcoming fiftieth-anniversary celebration on CBS, which I couldn't watch as I was someone who lived in the world without a TV or a CBS Access Pass. I could not have imagined, whining in my bedroom in 1972, that not only would I someday not have a TV (a version of hell I wouldn't dare to even conjure—what horrific sin would I have had to commit for someone to take that away from me?), but that this crew would be reuniting and that my mother and I would be communicating via a computer. Younger readers might also need to have it explained that summer used to be a TV-less desert, whereas the new world order is reversed. Heading into June, we're lousy with binge opportunities, thanks to premium cable's and streaming services' seemingly scattershot but most assuredly strategic and definitely torturous "season" scheduling; I am often wistful for the relative tumbleweeds.

It was during this 1970s period of concerted and constant TV watching that I was indoctrinated as an American consumer, as per TV's mission. Without a remote or mute button or the will to stop watching for one moment, I was fed a heavy diet of ads and embraced it, a hungry and willing hostage. As far as I was concerned, the ads were part of the program, even though I'd occasionally use them as a bathroom break. Today's TV viewers can't boast about knowing all the words to the Burger King anthem ("Two hundred million people, no two are quite the same . . .") or be quick with a fitting tagline—"It's Shake 'n Bake, and I helped!"; "Hey, Kool-Aid!"; "Nothing says lovin' like something from the oven!" I spoke in commercial-ese and believed every message that was sent my way. Commercials instilled in me the hope that the right shampoo would solve all of my hair, and consequently some existential, problems. But those same Pantene ads featuring the long, impossibly lush and stick-straight locks motivated me to dry my wavy hair with an asbestos-spewing hair dryer for thirty minutes every night and then train myself not to move my head while sleeping (leading to unpredictable and inconsistent hair texture and a chronically sore neck). And sexism was de facto in almost every ad. Only moms worried about stubborn stains or what to make for dinner. I still think of my dad cracking wise in response to the ad for the Playtex 18 Hour Bra, shilled by the voluptuous Jane Russell: "What the hell happens after eighteen hours?"

At the age of fifty-two, after at least two if not three decades without thinking about it, I was able to perform the Life cereal commercial, original rhythm intact, as an impromptu one-person show for an audience of one on a long car ride where someone on the radio said something that made me think of the plot of that ad, and out it came:

Scene: Three young boys at a kitchen table. A large box of Life cereal is placed in the center.

Boy #1: What's that?

Boy #2: Some cereal. S'posed to be good for you.

Boy #1: You try it?

Boy #2: I'm not gonna try it. You try it.
Boy #1: I'm not gonna try it.
Boy #2: Let's get Mikey!
Boy #2: Yeah! He won't do it. He hates everything.
Boy #1: He likes it! Hey, Mikey!

I could have just gone to YouTube and transcribed this clip, you might be thinking, but I assure you that this dialogue spewed unbidden from my mouth, like the pea soup from Linda Blair's Regan MacNeil. This is a testament to the vulnerability and sponginess of young brains (would that I had watched TV in Japanese or Arabic) as well as the hours spent in front of the TV in order to see that ad enough times to commit every word, breath, and inflection to memory—for life. Like riding a bike. The actor who played Mikey, not incidentally, became the subject of an urban legend in later years, wherein it was believed by many that he actually died from ingesting Pop Rocks in combination with soda pop, causing his stomach to explode. If like me you knew all the words to that ad, you know why the legend sums up our youth in such a perfect little way. Nancy Miller again: "There's nothing like death to offer the kind of closure that allows for shapely storytelling." Even if that death was at one time greatly exaggerated.

I was an easy mark for "act now" deals. The record albums with the scrolling titles were most compelling of all, and I convinced my mother to write a check for $3.99 for the eclectic 1977 *Muskrat Love* double compilation album because it featured my favorite songs, such as "Car Wash," "More than a Feeling," "Love Theme from *A Star Is Born* (the Barbra Streisand iteration)," "You Don't Have to Be a Star," and "Tonight's the Night," as well as the Captain and Tennille title track (admittedly my least favorite of the bunch, compounded by the album's cover art, which consisted of a hideous primary-color depiction of two cartoon muskrats holding paws on a bench). Even though I was well acquainted with the original versions of these top forty hits, I never realized that the "Muskrat Love" renditions were performed by different, unknown people basically doing karaoke.

Some of the messages in between shows that also went straight to my psyche included those that didn't send subliminal messages to buy things or how to be a lady but hoped to change my behavior for a lifetime. I didn't need a graphic visual of a person speaking via voice box to get me to avoid cigarettes. The "Kick the Habit" campaign, which was signified by a spry person carrying out an acrobatic heel click, was powerful enough. Despite (or to spite) what I believe is an inherently addictive personality, I have smoked less than a pack of cigarettes in my life, most of those in my twenties and in the year I lived in San Francisco trying on a different personality. Likewise, Woodsy Owl ensured that I gave way more than a hoot. I believe all polluters—especially whoever these vulgarians are who simultaneously commit three crimes by 1) attending to oral hygiene in public, 2) with single-use flossers, and then 3) dropping them on the ground—should be sentenced to the same fate that sea animals are when they ingest them in the ocean. And despite my anti-animation stance, *Schoolhouse Rock* did burrow its way in. While I am still fuzzy on the legislative process, I am a grammar fascist, not least of which includes the proper use of conjunctions and adverbs. As a librarian who traffics in Boolean operators, I can go on for a good long time about the function of conjunctions. And if there's one jingle that has proven to be a lasting truth, it's that America *is* baseball, hot dogs, apple pie, and Chevrolet.

Mostly with the commercials, though, I couldn't get enough of the food porn. The way a choosy mom (especially if she was fully fledged Mouseketeer Annette Funicello) spread peanut butter on a slice of bread with a gratuitous flourish; the textures and transformations involved in Pillsbury poppin' fresh biscuits; chocolate stirred or poured from an impractical height onto some other food or into the shape of a candy bar. Even the Nestea plunge had me suddenly, hysterically parched. But just like real porn, TV ads lie. That was not real butter, it turns out, baked into the valley across the top of a loaf of Home Pride bread. It takes way more than three licks to get to the center of a Tootsie Pop. And the two scoops of raisins were all rock hard and at the bottom of the cereal box. After school during one of my first turns as a latchkey eleven-year-old, I attempted to make my own chocolate cascade from scratch by placing a mini Nestlé Crunch bar directly into a tiny eight-ounce Revereware copper-bottom butter-melting pan over the stove's gas flame. Not yet conversant with the double boiler or physics, I was shocked when rather than melting into a beautiful, spoonable-into-my mouth confection, it caught on fire and left a perfect black tattoo of itself on the bottom of the pan, which I hid under my bed for about a year before throwing it out. Also, the Ginsu knife did *not* cut a beer can in half. But sex and ads sell, so to hell with the truth. The *Mad Men* series finale captured the supremacy of advertising (and consumers' losing battle with it) with the blindingly brilliant alternative origin story of the Coca-Cola ad that brought together a generation in perfect harmony.

As soon as the credits rolled on the final prime-time selection on any given weeknight, it was bedtime, full stop. Forty years on, 11 p.m. on weeknights remains a vestigial marker, inducing fluttery thoracic panic if the hour has arrived and my teeth remain unbrushed. I confess it was not much of a sacrifice, because the local news offered me nothing. But it required shifting positions, from a horizontal one on the carpet, or in a fiddlehead coil, squished onto the loveseat with my mother, some limb usually asleep, to an upright one and suddenly, after the lull of hours of mental escape, I was that much closer to having to wake up at a punishing hour and contend with real adolescent life. My mother had the luxury of remaining in her viewing position, interested as she was in the news, but really biding her time until *The Tonight Show*.

Many of my generation and older report a Pavlovian response to the peppy horns ushering in Johnny Carson. As an obedient and self-regulating child, the autonomous response I had to Doc Severinsen's theme was a cold pit in my solar plexus. I became anxious because I was hearing it and was therefore still awake, and that mental state kept me alert and bushy-tailed, sometimes for hours. After my mother had gone to bed (Johnny was on for ninety minutes! I would definitely flunk my trig test!), I listened to my father's distant snores and the minutes flipping on my yellow alarm clock as I stared unblinking at the orange glow that came from deep within that evil messenger.

But occasionally, when I felt the dread coming on, before *Tomorrow* came on, I would shuffle back to the TV room and whine to my mother that I couldn't sleep. Without taking her eyes off the screen for fearing of missing a Don Rickles insult, she would absently stroke my hair with one hand (calming and simultaneously serving the straightening agenda) and hold a cigarette aloft with the other, the ash dangerously lengthening over her flammable housecoat. Falling asleep to innuendo-laden jokes that I half understood was peculiarly soothing.

Those were weeknights, and weeknight rules applied. On weekends, all bets were off. Just as I was an early adopter of *Sesame Street*, I was also there—inappropriately at age ten—for the debut of *Saturday Night Live*. It was 11:29 p.m., so I should have been in bed, but given the aforementioned gestalt of the era, nary an eye was batted amongst my parents' friends at the prospect of me hanging around. Not that they noticed. I was inconspicuous and ninja-like, sneaking over to pick pepperoni off the congealing pizza on the coffee table and listening to George Carlin's opening monologue (which was actually dispersed throughout the show in discursive bits, four-plus minutes of which were devoted to God's imperfections). He was compelling physically, not just because of the beard and long hair, but because of his exaggerated voices and facial expressions that I see in retrospect were imprinted onto my dad. My father was a big Carlin fan, owned his *FM & AM* and *Class Clown* albums, and I am certain that my unsuitable early exposure to both Carlin and my dad's salty vernacular is the reason I feel so at home around cursing, atheists, and truth-to-power comedy.

SNL is a rare program that has been a travel companion along this winding journey. While I have not watched it religiously over the last forty years, I have seen the majority of sketches from each season and have a good sense of who the Not Ready for Prime Time Players were at any given time and even remember Robert Downey Jr. and Julia Louis-Dreyfus briefly among them. Not long ago, I heard Lorne Michaels say in an interview that when people relate their memories of the show, it's usually from their high school period. For me, the most memorable skits and catchphrases came along when I was in middle school, which I like to think means that I was smarter than my peers in ways that really mattered. Amy, my fellow Miss California and Kurt Thomas leotard viewer, and I liked to respond to most questions with either, "I don't know, Babs, but I do know this," or "Jane, you ignorant slut." In my twenties and thirties, when I went out on Saturday nights, and if I made it home before 1:00 a.m., *SNL* served as a soft crash landing. If I missed it, I might not fill the gaps until years later via a random rerun or a YouTube snippet. If you had told me, in 1992, that my tipsy Saturday night ritual would one day become a very sober Sunday morning one semi-enjoyed along with the *New York Times* crossword, I would not have been able to understand a word you were saying.

The fact that *SNL* and my generation have grown up together creates a loyalty for many of us toward Lorne Michaels—even when he disappeared from his exec producer's desk for five years—and the show's expected hits and misses. (It's live! They just wrote it three days ago! It's been on since Carter was president!) The longevity of certain shows–*The Simpsons, 60 Minutes, The Tonight Show*—and their constant, sometimes grating, presence is like a marriage, and we forgive a lot.

Tweenagedom is almost always a vulnerable and dramatic period, and like any normal kid, I experienced the obligatory fear and self-doubt about everything from killer bee invasions, airline hijackings, oil crises, kidnapping, and hostage taking, to not being picked during the Hitchhiker at the dozen or so disco roller rink bar mitzvah parties I attended. Political news might have alarmed the adults in my life, but it didn't interest or make sense to or seem relevant to me; therefore, news coverage of current events was the equivalent of static on the TV. One instance, however, broke through my blissful ignorance. In the summer of 1974, my parents carted me along on a short vacation to Long Island to visit friends. Our stay happened to include August 9, the day that Richard Nixon resigned. While I was too young to be aware of the hanky-panky or anything going on in the world of politics or the world, period, it was 1974, and even though I eschewed news programs, one could not escape at least knowing that there was something called the Vietnam War and another thing called Watergate. Both conjured childish and dramatic images, the former probably quite accurately, and the latter certainly in no way germane to the issue at hand, though some might argue that a giant Munsters-like iron gate impossibly damming a giant oceanic wave is actually an apt representation of what was going on.

My parents were politically liberal, or at least had the trappings of such, what with one of those iconic photos of the direly consulting profiles of Jack and Bobby Kennedy mounted prominently in our hallway, a peace symbol candle, a long-haired friend, and the McGovern button they pinned on my coat in '72 which earned a thumbs-up from Miss Levy/Ms. Mintz. On the night of the televised resignation speech, while I sat extremely close to the TV watching *The Waltons* by myself, I smelled what I (years) later understood to be weed coming from a distant room that my mom and her friend had repaired to. When presidential show time approached, everyone joined me around the TV, the menfolk with Schlitz bottles in hand, their wives oddly quiet. It's not possible to separate my own memories of Tricky Dick and Pat boarding the plane from the thousands of images plastered over any visual history of the twentieth century, but I was "there" and remember at least having an inkling that it was a big deal.

While TV had never been good to Nixon, that night he made the best of it. And it's hard to argue that it wasn't a moment of togetherness keenly remembered by a good number of people. Even though it was yet to be coined the end of the "long national nightmare," the sentiment was forged in that broadcast. Though the Mets and Pirates continued playing in Pittsburgh while this was going on and remained an option on one channel, more than one hundred million people watched the same images on all the other networks. The last time we'd all gathered in such numbers was for the moon landing five years earlier. It was one of the last such unified moments of the network era. In stark contrast, I think of the maniacal channel hopping we engage in now when big news events occur. On election night 2012, groups of people gathered across the country, someone inevitably shouting, "Go to ABC, quick! Diane Sawyer's drunk!" because they had just received a Twitter tip. We try to cobble together a full picture of the event, scrambling to watch every channel and crowd-source every social media play-by-play at once. It might feel exciting and immediate, but it is not quite the same electrifying experience as gathering around the electronic hearth in a virtual huddle. In 2016 we actually screamed at each other to change the channel to the one that had a better answer, a more hopeful outlook, as if the one we had been watching was suddenly deemed broken and unreliable. Not only was that illogical (desperate), but it was that very splintering off—the bubble behavior—that supposedly got us into the boiling vat we found ourselves in by the end of that evening. If the Clinton vs. Trump campaign had been broadcast on three TV and zero social networks, how might things have been different? Don't answer. It's a rhetorical question.

6

Luke & Laura & Sam & Diane

The Nixon resignation spectacle would prove to be an aberration for me, and my attention to politics went on hiatus for nearly two more decades. The fact that Chevy Chase's impression of a clumsy Gerald Ford intentionally disregarded anything about the president's physical appearance or vocal mannerisms corresponded with my lack of attention to that fill-in president as well as the one that came after him (Carter takeaway: peanuts, inflation, and Christianity). Reagan's two terms covered a long period of my adolescence through which I remained ignorant and apolitical. To wit, on the grey morning after Reagan's election to his first term in 1980, I met my friend Karen to walk to school. She looked stricken and went in for a hug, which was not our usual greeting. I waited for more information. Whatever she said next led me to understand that she was upset because of the election outcome. I was not unaware of the election or the outcome, but I was personally unmoved. I quickly matched her affect, however, knowing that it mattered to her, and to her politically aware and active parents, and somehow it mattered to the world (and even affected the ensuing content on my beloved TV without my knowing it). But I was faking it.

Though I remained steadfastly me-focused, once I entered high school, my viewing habits changed, and TV's place in my life took on new roles. Not so much the amount I consumed—it was still a central feature of my consciousness and the piece of furniture I looked at more than any other—but the way I watched it shifted.

From 1980 to 1983, the schedule went like this on an average weekday:

- 7:00–8:00 a.m.: showered; Cinnamon Life (or similar) cereal; fiddled with hair for the remaining time, arranging the barrettes at the socially correct angle. *Good Morning America* on in the background while my mom (with whom I shared the bathroom) applied her makeup. Her rummaging in her makeup case is a Proustian touchstone.
- 8:30–8:50: Walked to school with Karen and Emily, often rehashing previous evening's fare, for example, *Square Pegs* (drastic uptick in use of "gag me with a spoon" and "grody" throughout school day), *Happy Days* (past its prime, though, honestly, I'd always chafed against the odd casting of what I felt was an asexual sex symbol in Arthur Fonzarelli), *Laverne and Shirley*.
- 8:15 a.m.–2:30 p.m.: School. Scant recollection other than abovementioned opportunities for trendy parlance and footwork (unregulated shlemieling and shlimazelling down high school hallways slowed traffic flow between class periods).
- 2:30–4:00: Cheerleading practice. Our coach was bananas about *Cheers*. My squadmates and I started watching to up our sophistication quotient, as we admired Mrs. Hunter as

well as her totally cute history-teacher husband. Practice time compromised by dogged repetition of theme song and at least one instance of breaking into school cafeteria kitchen to steal industrial-size can of La Choy Chow Mein Noodles (lack of discipline reflected in our game day performances).
- 4:30–6:00: Ostensible completion of math homework in front of MTV.

Modifications during the off season:

- 2:30–3:00 p.m.: Rush to Earl's Drugs for candy to get to Karen's house in time for *General Hospital*; french and fishbone braiding of one another's hair. (These days, as a nostalgic quinquagenarian, I am reminded of this afternoon ritual by the small clique of blue jays in the tree outside my living room window that convene daily around 3:00–4:00 p.m., like raucous, entitled adolescents).
- 4:00–5:00: *Mike Douglas Show*; critiquing and admiring of celebrities.

It was still a privileged and carefree life I led. But one starts to observe scheduled activities entering the picture and choices being made—whom I spent time with and how we spent the time together. Some activities replaced television, and that was maybe a good thing. But TV still filled in all the unscheduled spaces, other than meals and sleeping.

The pairing of food and TV is a potential dissertation unto itself for anyone who wants to take it on. Eating and TV have always gone together as naturally as chocolate and peanut butter—"two great tastes that taste great together!" That chicken-and-egg philosophical conundrum posited by the 1970s Reese's ads—Hey you got your chocolate in my peanut butter! No, you got your peanut butter in my chocolate!—is responsible for my highly empathic nature, where I inherently position myself at the vantage point of even diametrically opposed arguments to be able to mediate a workable and creative solution. Nope, just joking.

The guidelines around eating in my house were generally as rigid as those around watching television, that is, not rigid, the earlier tale of my defensive lawn snacking notwithstanding. I loved going to Wegmans with my mother on the weekly shopping trip from the time I was small enough to sit in the cart until I went off to college. Mom took care of all the essential things a family needs, and I took care of the rest, tossing in assortments of Keebler and Sara Lee provisions, Snack Pack pudding cups, Snackin' Cake mix, Pop-Tarts, Cinnamon Life, and Flintstone Chewable Vitamins. More often than not, our two shopping lists overlapped, given that Oscar Mayer Wieners, Kraft Macaroni and Cheese, and Hamburger Helper were the stuff of weeknight meals for us and also checked off the boxes of delicious and processed (which constituted one box, really). Food marketing people should not underestimate the decision-making and once-removed buying power of a preteen girl in the American family, though this may have been more marked in the more restrictive gender roles era of the 1970s. It was the ideal activity for a girl to feel like she was helping her mom do important adult domestic work. And for a fastidious girl kid like me who would voluntarily reorganize the canned food in the cupboard so that all the like foods were grouped together and the labels accommodatingly faced out, coupon cutting and organizing were irresistible adjunct activities.

I've already covered the obvious entry in this category, the TV dinner, and I've mentioned the ravioli/Miss America and *Wizard of Oz*/egg custard traditions. But to be watching TV without also having a snack nearby at any time felt like an incomplete activity. When I got home from school, I made a beeline for the thoughtfully curated snack cupboard and got to work. Those sleeves of Oreos (or Hydrox) weren't going to eat themselves. Away we went to the TV together, happily and completely guilt-free on all counts. Obviously this was not a behavior unique to me. My friends and I devoured our Earl's Drugs candy booty—Sky Bars, Broadway strawberry licorice rolls, Mallo Cups, Smarties, you name it, we tried it—in front of whoever's TV on which we were watching *General Hospital.* Karen's freezer was a known source of the highly coveted, extra-large Wegmans chocolate chip cookies. Emily's household introduced me to Haagen-Dazs.

Everybody equates eating with TV. TV itself fosters and reinforces the connection—in fact it is an essential ingredient in its purpose. Selling products is its numero uno priority, and the body image impact is very complicatedly related. I won't go so far as to blame the TV industry for the obesity epidemic or eating disorders or compromised self-esteem the way cancer survivors (rightfully and successfully) blamed Philip Morris, but I just put that association in front of you, and you can't unread it. Who could we sue anyway? Philo Farnsworth? The FCC? At the very least, we can all agree that TV (and all other popular media) had a hand in forming our national standards of beauty.

A bit of a side note, but somewhat connected to the whole persuasion-seduction-manipulation-mendacious-gaslighting operation: While we watched with our mouths full, we frequently saw images of the actual foods we were eating (ads work!). Remember my fixation with food porn TV ads? I alluded to this delusion earlier: Somehow eating the object of my consumption never matched the TV image. The chocolate was not as glistening and the cookie not as crisp with flakes gracefully leaping into the air when snapped in half. But more to the deeper point, we also saw, butting right up against those ads for Stouffer's French Bread Pizza and Tato Skins, the bodies we were supposed to have—Brooke Shields in her Calvins; CoverGirl Cheryl Tiegs; the Enjoli super-lady with come-hither frying pan. Remember, this was the 1980s, and while we are all familiar with the mixed and equally powerful messages served up by all media in the 21st century, in the 1980s, it felt like a new wave, like a Technicolor dreamcoat of sparkle paint had been lacquered over the suede earth tones of the sixties and seventies. Excess and acquisition were championed—finally! Jane Fonda and *Cosmo* magazine covers posited a body type that we should all aspire to. On a parallel track, the booming economy and the rise of celebrity chefs made eating rich and fancy foods a favorite (or desired) activity. We were tempted and lured by images, both coming from media, of the rich foods and the lithe figures; a battle waged in our own brains and bodies: Eat this! Look like this! No, eat this! But still look like this! Everything felt feverish and manic, as if we were all vicariously coked up, aerobicizing to Olivia Newton John in our leg warmers while jamming zero-calorie, fat-free, pesto-infused, air-popped snack balls into our faces.

So in the face of all this bounty, we had to take action, impose psychic and behavioral restraining orders. In my household, guilt and shame crept into our daily eating habits in a much more intrusive manner than it did into our TV-watching habits. We never really said—any maybe never even thought—anything as severe as, "We should watch less TV." I don't know what precipitated my parents' embarking on fad dieting, but I have to believe that it coincided with the time that mainstream culture and its mouthpiece, TV, started telling us we were supposed to be thin. We (all of Western civilization, but I can tell only the story of my family) therefore craved guilt-free eating more than ever, and my parents must have felt they had to put a harsh rule into effect. At one point they followed a mono diet that involved, on alternate days, hot dogs, sauerkraut, eggs, and grapefruit salad, the kind that came in a gigantic jar, punctuated with maraschino cherries throughout. It goes without saying that this was insane (and I understand from Google that mono food diets are still a thing). I was not allowed to touch their stash during the prescribed diet period, which of course was all I wanted to do. There were other diets, like when my mom tried Weight Watchers, which sold its own horrible food, including the double chocolate chip cookies made with egg whites only that had the texture and taste of pumice stones. And then my dad invented one for himself that consisted of Triscuits, apples, and fat-free yogurt. My point is, it was crazy, the eighties were crazy, my parents got caught up in the crazy, and ipso facto, as a member of the household and the culture, I got some crazy on my shirt.

I was still eating varied, colorful, as-seen-on-TV foods guilt-free for the most part as I watched my parents try these experiments, not feeling any judgment about my own eating or body shape one way or the other. But that would soon change, and my precipitating event, of course, was puberty and then going off to college (the things were only two years apart for me, which is not all that uncommon but seems tragic in retrospect, and now I think all teens should take a gap year not only from school but from the media just to settle into their bodies and love themselves before going to college and spending the rest of their lives combating the unrealistic messages callously thrown at them). As one who has gone from eating delectable chemicals to a short-lived sampling of collegiate disordered eating to a balance of healthy plus pleasure-only foods who can no longer abide the taste of the Hostess HoHo I once extolled, I can say with conviction that I miss those days of clueless, hedonistic eating quite a bit.

While I was not a full-fledged couch potato, TV and I were close to inseparable for the duration of my life under my parents' roof. I felt remorseful only to the extent that my dad reminded me that I should be outside, but there was no TV outside, so I didn't really know what I should do out there. Occasionally I hit a tennis ball against the garage door, one that had glass panes at the top, and I'm not sure how my dad let this happen, given his adamant attitude about my channel-changing behavior. Maybe he was just glad I was outside and knew that replacing a few small windows would be easier than replacing the channel changer dial (I never broke a pane or the channel changer).

It might not be necessary to explain that while I was a normal red-blooded kid who had a requisite list of ever-changing ranked crushes in a secret page of my Literature Arts spiral notebook, I did not interact in anything but a platonic way with the opposite sex for most of my teen years. My first kiss, if you can even call it that, was under duress at my first boy-girl party in sixth grade while playing Seven Minutes in Heaven, a now-quaint gambit wherein one teen is forced into a closet with another insecure member of the teen human race and of the opposite sex (the only option; it was the 1970s) for an eternity. There were no instructions for what you did in there, but it was customary to at least make a half-hearted attempt to do something of a quasi-romantic or fondling nature. I got paired with Eric M., a nice boy for whom I had nothing but neutral feelings. In retrospect, I suspect he was the boy version of me in terms of sex appeal and social standing, where the word "neutral" applies again in each case. When I picture him now, I can see his senior yearbook portrait, him in an olive green tee shirt with a contrasting piping around the collar and the mandatory unnatural head tilt. I can remember my own flop sweat upon entering the closet but also the mutual shrugging followed by a gentle, dry and chaste peck on the lips. His lips were pleasingly soft, and his breath odor was detectable but neither good nor bad, just honest. Maybe we sat there nervously laughing for a few minutes before opening the door, or maybe we exited before the time was up, peer protestations be damned.

The next day, my parents went to a real estate open house, as they were interested in trading up, and they brought me along, always respectfully seeking my gut kid feelings along with their own financial ones. The house we were looking at was, coincidentally, Eric M.'s. Of course the M family was not present, and I enjoyed my secret in a dry and chaste way, feeling much more grown up than I had the previous day. This house would do, I concluded. We lived there for the rest of my middle school and high school life, and for some strange reason, I never thought of it as Eric M.'s house after that day. The room we ended up calling the library because of its wall of built-in bookshelves was designated the TV room (no more den for us; we had moved on up). It had been Eric's brother's room. I remember seeing it at the open house and there just being a mattress on the floor along with the dangerous aura of older teenage boy. From 1977 through half of 1983, I spent more time in that room than in any other in the house, after my bedroom.

There were no other kisses after that until I was a senior in high school. By alphabetic virtue I was paired with Felix at the two-person lab table in physics class. He was tall and brown-skinned and was on the football team and was not an academic superstar and was a bit of a pathological liar. We could not have been less each other's type, but from the first day of physics class, he began surreptitiously pushing me with his elbow so that I had to push back to keep from sliding off my chair. This garden-variety flirting device led to the obvious next step, which was his asking me to study with him for the Regents exam. I invited him to my house on a weekday after school, and my parents did an Oscar-worthy job of masking their shock when I came home with not only a boy but a really strapping one wearing a sleeveless, midriff-baring sweatshirt. He invited me to his house on a weeknight when his entire family was on vacation (I didn't question the oddness or risk of this). By weeknight, Felix meant, like, midnight. It must have been an acute case of senioritis, because I schemed to make this happen. I kept my bike hidden outside the garage and waited until my mother finally went to bed. It was the one time I strayed from the late-weeknight ritual of anxiety-watching *The Tonight Show* and was so out of my wheelhouse that I remember the exact tee shirt and sweat pants I wore as I rode my ten-speed Columbia bike through the dark streets of my quiet suburb to Felix's house. When my dad encouraged/chastised me to go outside, I doubt this is what he had in mind. A tiny TV blared Doc Severinsen's horns just as Johnny welcomed the audience back from a commercial break, and Felix welcomed me into his attic bedroom. A clock radio simultaneously blared the Eurythmics' "Sweet Dreams Are Made of This." Like Elaine, I promise I am not yadda-yadda-ing over the best parts. Honestly, those were the most interesting elements of that very late evening.

Though it's difficult for me to reconcile a girl who would undertake such an illicit activity with the same one who was usually babysitting on Saturday nights, I can see you rolling your eyes, muttering, "There's a shocker." True enough, for as the 1950s era Neapolitan teenaged Lenu's voiceover describes in HBO's *My Brilliant Friend*, my life, too, "was splendid but low on events." But I'll have you know, even babysitting provided opportunities for the wild child inside me. No, I didn't have my boyfriend over (because I was still about a decade away from having one) to ransack the family's liquor cabinet (because I wouldn't have bothered to look for one), but I did employ deceit and engage in petty theft. As food always was and continues to be my central vice, I would scour the fridge and cupboards for pilferable foods—the open bag of Nestlé Semisweet Chocolate Morsels, the half-empty gallon of Sealtest Heavenly Hash, the partially rummaged boxes of Mister Salty pretzels and Frosted Mini-Wheats. Anything whose remaining amount would go undetected or misremembered was in play. I once went so far as to shave off a half inch slice of a leftover Italian sub. I would have made a great balaclava-clad safe cracker in another life.

When our neighbor asked me to corral the kids upstairs while the adults had a revelrous repast downstairs, I ferried full meals from the kitchen to the dad's large and TV-outfitted office like a waitress in a sports bar. Baby Suzanne was content to wetly smash her Pepperidge Farm goldfish in her portable high chair while Daniel and I sat with our plates of roast beef and potatoes in front of us on the floor watching *The Muppet Show*. Daniel, aged five or eight or seven, was, of course, more interested in the TV than his food, so while he sat slack-jawed before Fozzie Bear, I speared one of his potatoes and tucked it into my cheek, assuming he was none the wiser. When his mother came in later to check on us, Daniel blurted, without even looking at me, "I was watching the *television*, and the next thing I knew, she had eaten one of my *potatoes*!" I supposed I deserved it, and betrayed though I felt, I had to admire his poker face during the incident. The strongest association with babysitting, though, was the immersive *Love Boat/Fantasy Island* bloc that usually took us from the kids' bedtime to the return of the parents. Because I was usually ready to be free of the kids long before 9:00 p.m., I would sometimes change the stove clock to reflect one hour later to prove that it was time for bed. If you're thinking that seems extreme, remember that it was much quicker and quieter to do this in the analog age. This worked with most of my charges (though bedtime wrangling no matter the hour was always stressful and hardly worth the $1–$3 per hour I was earning), but obviously not with Daniel, who was smarter than me in numerous ways.

7

Beaucoup et Rien

It wasn't just my life that changed now that I was a member of the employed class. TV content, too, reflected the priorities of the 1980s that revolved around money and hideous fashions. Though Matt Zoller Seitz would disagree, I contend that the golden age was behind us and that we had entered the gold-plated age. Many were dazzled by the prime-time soaps *Dynasty*, *Dallas* (who shot JR? Bing Crosby's daughter!), and *Knots Landing*. For my part, the 1980s had a few salvageable artifacts: *The Cosby Show*, *Cheers*, *Family Ties*, *The Wonder Years*, *Mork and Mindy*. As for the latter, it bears mentioning that Mork's appearance on *Happy Days* seemed more like jumping the shark than the actual shark jumping, but starring in his own sitcom was an act I deemed perfectly acceptable. These couldn't be further from the hard-livin' Americana reenactments I'd enjoyed a few years earlier, but I was forced to move with the times. Like Seitz, my husband—a mere three years my junior—is more connected with the 1980s, probably due to the fact that he spent his formative (TV) years in Europe, where he watched *Space 1999* dubbed in Italian and vividly associates his

US homecoming with the jubilant discovery of Gary Coleman on *Different Strokes*.

And it wasn't just content on the networks that looked and acted differently. Much more dramatic was format and delivery. Cable TV had arrived.

"For most of the history of civilization, there was nothing like TV," wrote technology journalist Farhad Manjoo in the *New York Times* in 2017. "It was a really odd moment in history to have so many people watching the same thing at the same time. As the broadcast era changed into one of cable and then streaming, TV was transformed from a wasteland into a bubbling sea of creativity." Let's break this down. First of all, no wonder TV had such a hold on me—it was a wasteland! I was a female, American teen, a species that naturally enjoys unnatural foods and hair textures, so it follows that I would also enjoy highly commercialized junk TV fare. Except we all know that the 1961 Minow wasteland speech was the screed of an elitist egghead and Cold War apparatchik. The wasteland label is now as ridiculously archaic as Sylvester Graham's zany idea that a vegan diet quelled sexual desire, when everyone knows that graham crackers themselves are an aphrodisiac, especially if the graham cracker itself is the object of your desire.

Now, think about this part: The "people watching the same thing at the same time" facet of TV was unique to only two and half generations in US history—mine, my parents', and my half-watching grandparents'. It still happens occasionally in our current day, like with the Super Bowl, which is why the ads are so expensive and long. It (the-same-thing-at-the-same-time phenomenon) is also the aspect that compels me the most. I will concede that because programmers felt pressure to please everybody, plots could be simplistic and characters flat. But it was also an opportunity for impact, to wake people up. Socially progressive, envelope-pushing shows teemed in the 1960s and 1970s—in addition to those already waxed about, I have yet to mention the groundbreaking *Smothers Brothers Comedy Hour*, which kept the CBS standards and practices outfit on their toes for a couple of years. And even more than that, the shared cultural experience was a moment of imagined unity. To be on the same page with people for a brief moment felt easy and righteous. It was like living in a suburb where everyone went to the same school, grocery store, and two restaurants, as opposed to a city with a thousand choices for each. I grew up in such a suburb, both onscreen and off, almost completely unaware for much of my early life—for better or worse—that there was anything but perfect harmony in the world.

As my obvious soulmate, Amy Poehler, writes in her memoir, *Yes Please*, "That's why my parents went to a *M*A*S*H* party and watched the last episode in real time. There was no next-day *M*A*S*H* cast Google hangout. . . . Things happened in real time and you watched them together. There was no rewind." She goes on to talk about her relationship with TV and HBO and MTV and how she ate in front of the TV and watched things she was too young for and how her lower-middle-class family got HBO even though they couldn't really afford it. I can deduce from Amy's micro-chronicle of her life with TV that my experience is not just limited to a very small slice of the citizenry (i.e., not just people born in 1965; Amy is six years my junior), so I feel even more emboldened to chronicle mine so discursively.

As for me and *M*A*S*H*, yes, thankfully that one is in my canon and categorized as golden age. The finale was especially moving for me, because it happened during my last year in high school, and I was already nursing a melodramatic teen-tinged angst about leaving everything behind. Also, something about the relationship between Hawkeye and BJ reminded me of my dad and his best friend, Ward (aka the next-door husband). Even though they weren't saying any goodbyes (though they actually did, when a year later my parents traded both up and out and moved out of state, so maybe I was prescient), it felt like that TV farewell foretold a world of endings. It was the same sadness I felt when I believed Carol Burnett to be giving her final ear tug.

As for the "bubbling sea of creativity" that the *New York Times*' Farhad Manjoo describes, it took some time. HBO, while exciting in its debut (arriving on our doorstep circa 1979), it was initially a second-run movie distribution outlet. That which cable wrought did not quite match the dumb-looking fake-wood-paneled box acquired from the local cable company that sat on the bottom shelf of our TV cart, its plastic push buttons (once the edge of tech innovation) similar to those of the blender. It so wanted to be furniture, too. There were thirty-seven numbers in three rows (it lacked a "1"), and one had to select a row with a dial and then depress the corresponding button. Naturally, there was a proper way to push these buttons, according to my father, so that I didn't damage the thing and end up incurring damage fees. (Were they coming to take it back? How would they—or he—know if I pushed two buttons at the same time to see if I could, who knows, make contact with a satellite space station?) But this injunction quashed any question of adorning the thing with puffy stickers.

The main reason to succumb to the unusual habit of paying for TV shows was to be able to tell your neighbors you had cable. A close second was for HBO. Parents found CNN interesting, while kids took to Nickelodeon like neon on a Valley girl. The sister channel to HBO was Cinemax, also composed of movies, and I never could ascertain the difference between the two.

They were like Oreos and Hydrox, two products that looked essentially the same but revealed subtle differences in taste and that took turns being my favorite, depending on whichever I was consuming at the moment. By far the most pushed button on that box was the now-forgotten number between 2 and 37 that brought MTV into my life, on which more later. (My reptilian brain is now telling me that it was channel 20.) The transformation to a "bubbling sea of creativity" happened not over the course of a few months or years, but rather a few decades. It was gradual, like the proverbial frogs in boiling water, except that these frogs were not dead but rather woke and inspired by their new environment. A "bubbling sea" does sound potentially fetid and not quite safe for swimming, and it was that, too, at times over the evolutionary period. Cinemax later began airing adult, after-dark programming, earning itself the nickname Skinemax, which made me feel retroactively trashy on behalf of our family for having signed up. From the hot, thin soup of cable, production islands arose, providing the ideal conditions for the formation of the critically adored original programming with which we "have you seen?" each other in urgent tones in the early twenty-first century. Shows like *Curb Your Enthusiasm* and *Breaking Bad*, which provoke intense responses because people either loathe cringe-making social situations and graphic violence or are vicariously thrilled by both. And companies that used to just sell books online or send DVDs via the US postal service also became prestigious production hothouses, so that all those entities became nearly indistinguishable. But I'm rushing ahead of myself.

Back in the Reagan era, my parents bought a cottage on a rocky hill in Boothbay Harbor, Maine, which, even though I didn't spend all that much time there, is the locus of some significant screen memories from the 1980s. The monstrous TV from my childhood den made the trip all the way up there, as so many household goods do when they are still-operable relics that are fine for use in a second home. It fit in aesthetically with the leftover cottage wares from the previous owners—a floral upholstered loveseat with a scalloped back and wood-trimmed arm rests, a green Formica-and-chrome table with folding leaves on wheels, white wicker rocking chairs with faded cushions, lumpy mattresses, and the comforting yet melancholy, particularly New Englandy smell of old-but-not-rare books and desiccated starfish. The TV spent its last days there, and like a long-lived family pet who dies when you're no longer living at home, I don't remember any information about the moment it happened or even learning when or how it went, though I do feel sad retroactively and hope that it's living a good life on its farm upstate. I never got to say goodbye or give a nice gentle pat on its head to make up for all the cruel and usual punishment it received throughout its impressively long life of service.

The 1981 wedding of Prince Charles and Lady Diana Spencer may be one of the last images I saw on that screen. I was still in high school and thus still insular and ignorant. If I didn't give any mind to my own country's goings-on, you might wonder how I could be expected to care what was going on with British royals. I would say that we were in the era when the world stood still for such an event, that it was inescapable on your home TV set, but it is the same as it ever was four decades later. Because British royals, especially when pretty young princesses are being anointed, constitute TV manna the world over. It bears mentioning, given everything you know about me thus far, that Luke and Laura's wedding was only four months later and was also a very big (*General Hospital*) event. I don't remember being aware at the time of the obvious commonalities—Luke and

Lady Di shared the last name of Spencer. The Ice Princess jewel changed the Spencers and Cassadines forever, just as Diana did the royal family. And, to boot, Diana was a fan of the soap. Luke (Tony Geary) says he and Laura (Genie Francis) each received a congratulatory gift of champagne from Diana upon the occasion of their wedding. Such a gesture would seem within the bounds of ordinary for Meghan Markle, but in 1981 it was quite a bold and cheeky move for a princess.

Like childhood sweethearts, TV and I drifted apart when I went to college. We never broke up, but we saw a lot less of each other. I didn't miss TV or think about it much, despite our intimacy for nearly two decades. I was immersed in an entirely new world full of activities, leaving little time for hanging out with my old companion. Was it just my egocentric vantage point, or did I not miss much? TV seemed to be stagnating, not curious about learning new things or making new friends the way I was. I caught glimpses of TV in dorm lounges around campus—soap operas were excuses for social gatherings, and I occasionally sat on the arm of a stained sofa to watch a bit of *GH*, but I didn't recognize the new characters and quickly lost interest. I silently judged my peers who clearly didn't have the strength and maturity to let go.

What captured me for longer periods, of course, was MTV. It was still the era of veejays Martha Quinn, Nina Blackwood, JJ Jackson, and Alan Hunter, and we were at the age where caring about music was paramount, and the music video industry was at the age of caring about being visually captivating. Were you not spellbound by *Thriller*, *Material Girl*, *Wake Me Up before You Go-Go*, and *You Give Love a Bad Name*? Even the videos we loved to mock would hold our attention to the end—*We Built This City* and *Dancing in the Street*. (Go on, watch them now.) Then you'd have to wait to see what was coming up next. Binge watching was born. Everybody knew, from watching it four thousand times, whose solo was coming next in supergroup single *We Are the World*, making it physically impossible to not join Cyndi Lauper or exaggerate Bob Dylan's bit. Yes, young reader, you saw correctly: Bob Dylan—he who was too cool to collect his Nobel Prize was there along with Huey Lewis in a cheery, charity singalong.

The TV set was also useful as a device on which to watch Jane Fonda workout tapes—as if butt crunches could make a dent in the effects of three-hour cafeteria sessions as we avoided writing papers each night. My dorm-mates and I performed these on the beer-stiffened carpet of the communal lounge, amidst much ribbing from male passersby. As of this writing, Jane Fonda, for one, looks as good as she did in 1983, and I had always suspected that the sales of those VHS tapes, more than the effects of practicing the content, might have a bit to do with that. I was surprised to learn recently via the *Jane Fonda in Five Acts* documentary on HBO directed by Susan Lacy, that the workout tapes cottage industry came out of a need to raise money for political activist and Fonda husband Tom Hayden. I had always assumed they were just a selling out and bandwagon-jumping act of a radical-turned-capitalist, which was fine by me, and anyway a seal on the box indicating that proceeds were going to the Campaign for Economic Democracy would probably not have been fine by a ton of people who bought it. Had I known about the origin story when I was pelvic-thrusting in college, I might have seized the opportunity as a moment of self-righteous grandstanding and called it an act of civil disobedience. I say "might," but really, no I never would have; a) it was the eighties, and it was college, and we were self-centered and clueless, and b) I don't have an activist muscle in my body. I don't even think I really reconciled Hanoi Jane as being the same person as Fitness Jane until years after she basically invented aerobics (not to dismiss the impact of the charming spectacle of Richard Simmons), introduced the VCR, and married the billionaire founder of CNN.

My arrival on campus freshman year could be represented in a mental Instagram by my plush Samoyed family, James Taylor cassettes, and a mischaracterizing Grateful Dead poster. At the outset of my senior year, after a year abroad, I must have been feeling nostalgic for my old flame, because I showed up with a portable, mud-colored, nine-inch TV set (analogous to my portable record player and inching ever closer to my futuristic wireless, handheld TV) that picked up about 1.5 channels from the local broadcast region. As an example of one of those 1980s curvilinear consumer products, it was therefore further useless as a place atop which to rest any objects. I think I used it to watch *Moonlighting*. Once.

There were national and world events going on without my knowledge during my private liberal arts college bubble years. AIDS, South African apartheid, Chernobyl-esque disasters, and the Cold War seem to register. On campus, the issues we cared about in the moment (some of us to lesser degrees due to ignorance and self-absorption) were nuclear warfare, divestment from totalitarian regimes, and sexual harassment, though these have proven to be perennial campus issues. When I spent my junior year in Paris, a professor asked me in class what I thought about [insert headline-dominating, important, current political event here], and, having no informed opinion much less any understanding of the issue, I answered, "Beaucoup et rien." "Ah, très sage," he replied, either kindly, recognizing my stupidity, or genuinely considering me wise and appreciating my smartass answer. I got away with that one, but my aristocratic host family quizzed me nightly about issues of the day, hoping for an intelligent or at least authentic US perspective. Unfortunately for all of us, they did not get the student they were hoping for.

The family consisted of cartoonishly intimidating and formal parents, a high-school-aged daughter (who dressed and acted thirty) and two well-employed adult sons, all of who managed to come together every night for dinner, which was served at 9:00 p.m. at the earliest. "Je ne sais pas," I repeated in each session (my previously victorious "a lot and nothing" led to them only waiting for more), hoping that "I don't know" could be taken rhetorically rather than literally and that the family might nod in commiseration about the perplexing world we all live in. There was an incongruous television in their grand, chandeliered dining room, near the far end of the long banquet table, on an even more incongruous rolling metal cart. They had it set to a news channel. When the US launched airstrikes against Libya in 1986, my French host mother shrieked down the long narrow hallway toward my servants' quarters room, where I sat checking off all the English-subtitled movies I could see in the weekly *Pariscope*, in English (so I might finally understand something about my own country), "The US is at war!" as if to say, "This is what you deserve, you hopeless American."

The continuous inquisition in Paris was a harsh awakening for me. For a deliriously luxurious introduction month in the southern resort town of Biarritz, my host family was so warm and inviting that when I told them, as I petted their apricot poodle, Tifan, "Je veux baiser votre chien," my embarrassing error (my mini French-English dictionary had assured me that *baiser* meant only "to kiss") was greeted with a generous and delighted round of laughter from all. In that household, where I never saw a TV, we did not speak of politics once.

The relative TV dry spell continued for about a year after I graduated, until early 1988 when I stood in my friend's house looking at a small black-and-white TV on the kitchen counter, only because everyone else was. It was tuned to Fox. I had still been in college when the legendary fourth network was launched, and therefore it was a tree falling in a forest. I quickly became enamored of *The Tracey Ullman Show* in 1987, and embedded therein were the seedlings of the longest-running prime time TV show in the US, *The Simpsons*. I fell hard for Tracey (bright colors! funny lady! emancipated!) and started to get the taste for TV again, remembering how much unmitigated joy it brought me. *The Simpsons*, well, you know, deep respect, but it wasn't the lure for me. Even though we were in a post-cable era at this point, I thrilled to the idea of a fourth network, which seemed like the discovery of a new planet, so outside was it of everything I theretofore knew to be true in the universe. I felt duty-bound to pay attention to it, and perhaps it was the beginning of an awareness about myself as a meta-viewer. But more so, I was just a girl who wanted to have measured fun. And I did—*Married . . . with Children* (bring on the irreverence!), *MadTV*, *It's Garry Shandling's Show*, *The Ben Stiller Show*, *Ally McBeal, Beverly Hills, 90210* (much more on this later), *Melrose Place, Party of Five, The X-Files* (though I was far from fanatical, which is unusual for this show), *21 Jump Street* (though I was far from a fanatical Johnny Depp fan, which is unusual for this man). Later on, I dabbled in *Get a Life* and *Martin*, *Titus*, and *The Mindy Project* (comedians!), *That '70s Show* (my very own era, a period piece?), *NHL on Fox* (just kidding!), and, most recently *Raising Hope* (though it was delivered to me via Hulu and thus had little association with the network in my head).

I completely forget—and I doubt I'm alone in this—that the network that brought me all these pleasures is the same one that was founded by Rupert Murdoch and would change politics in the US 1992 election and beyond and whose news outlet would constitute a "different planet" upon which its viewers were living (per former President Barack Obama, in 2018). It's not quite the same as the impossibility of divorcing the before-and-after experience of Bill Cosby—such delight! such sorrow! It's more like Goofus and Gallant. How could two kids born of the same parents be so different, one so bad and one so good? Well, let's learn from it. Or just steer clear of and then disparage the bad one.

An incorrigible decadist, I have an annoying habit, like a children's encyclopedia on a remainders table, of generalizing, flattening, and assigning stereotypes to arbitrary time periods. The flattening brings into relief the stark contrasts that exist in historical retrospect, and I'm a sucker for that kind of sweeping imagery, even if some of it feels like pressing on a bruise. The 1980s visual collage flashes champagne kisses and caviar dreams, piles of cocaine, a skeletal AIDS patient, the floor of the New York Stock Exchange demonstrating elation and despair, shoulder pads, Reagan, Thatcher, Gorbachev, the crumbling Berlin Wall, Farm Aid. While these were actual, factual events, they are the easy, lazy associations. But easy, lazy associations are usually what TV captures, no matter the decade. Without these images, how else would we frame our lives and put a pin in our memories? It's no different than looking at the limited and curated photo albums from your childhood, those Kodak moments for the times of your life.

8

Cambridge 02138

In 1988 Oprah Winfrey pulled a wagon full of sixty-seven pounds of fat onto the stage of her talk show. I was incensed. Almost three decades later she confessed to regretting that stunt. "You can see that my ego is on flamboyant display," she told an interviewer. "I've had to pay the price for that moment over and over. I literally handed to the world on a fat wagon platter the story of 'Is She Fat?' 'Is She Thin?'" I didn't care about her tabloid troubles. What irked me was her pride in the fact that she had fasted for six weeks, because it was a negative message to send to viewers. At the time of the fat wagon episode, I was getting a master's degree in counseling psychology and had a vague but noble plan of working with women with eating disorders. The masses were already starting to worship Oprah, and I hated to think of all the women—and girls, especially—engaging in irresponsible copycat dieting. As for the wagon of fat, well, that was not only gratuitous and melodramatic (it made for great TV, of course), but because it was viscerally revolting, it seemed shaming, inviting the opposite of what Oprah spent most of her later career doing, which has been encouraging women to be their best selves. It seemed so obvious to me that I was right in my indignation, and maybe I was, but I couldn't find any joiners. I tried to get other women in my touchy-feely, self-esteemy graduate program to get enraged along with me, but no one else seemed to think it was so bad. I suppose they were all on diets of their own and wished they had their own wagons of fat to parade around with. Did I mention it was 1988? Did you read the earlier chapter about the grapefruit diet and the Cheryl Tiegs?

The late 1980s and early 1990s offered several galvanizing television events, most of which were widely considered to be weightier and more culturally defining than Oprah's fat wagon. The Clinton presidential campaign in 1992? I fell for it just as I had for the peanut butter and Pantene ads—smitten and bitten, hook, line, and sinker. MTV's Rock the Vote. The media gloss, Fleetwood Mac, peace love and understanding, communing with my generation. I felt what they engineered me to feel, just like shopping in Crate & Barrel does with its manipulative simple-chic pussy willow centerpieces, even though my most vivid recollection of the campaign was watching the election victory on my tiny curvilinear television in my tiny apartment alone. It was an experience that could literally be distilled down into a little box. (Six years later I watched the impeachment hearings on CNN at the gym.) Other events of the era that spring to mind: the Tiananmen Square massacre, the Gulf War, Rodney King and the LA riots, and the more prurient Lorena Bobbitt and Pamela Smart cases. I recently listened to an interview with a journalist on the sexual harassment beat who was asked by the interviewer to recap the Anita Hill story. I thought, "Why would anyone need a recap? That was so recent!" but it was twenty-eight years ago as I type this. That realization is not so much a prosaic "Wow, time flies!" as a testament to TV's uncanny ability to place significant events at the forefront, in the dock of the mind, always there, ready to access, as if they were just created the last time you turned on the computer.

The Real World, most people's first experience of reality TV if you don't count *Candid Camera* or *COPS*, appealed to me not because it felt "real" but because it was less plot-oriented than other shows. I never went in for the story arc. What happened in [insert title of TV show], you might want to know? "Nothing" is fine with me. I could have argued for George and Jerry's show about nothing pitch much better than George did. It's about characters. That's what people talk about when they talk about reality TV. Any writer will tell you there is a story, a dramatic tension in every program, some subtler than others. Otherwise, how do you keep people interested? They need something to happen, some obstacle for the characters to face and overcome or not. And I won't argue that my interest is not operating on that at some level. But just meeting new people, getting to know them, often getting to hate them is entertaining enough. For the first few minutes of a new character appearing on the screen, I am so distracted by reading the visual information that I am unable to pay attention to what is being said by anyone and usually am lost plot-wise. So, the less plot the better. I'm sure I am not unique, but it often feels so. When watching a new show on Netflix with Gerard and we're both immediately transfixed, I find out five minutes in that he is totally locked in with the plot while I am still looking at the protagonist's forehead or happily noticing that she, like me, has a slight lisp. Reality TV lost me before the end of season two of *Survivor*. I can't even watch *Top Chef* because of the heavy-hitting plots and story arcs. Cooking shows are now reality shows, and honestly, they all merge into one. Everyone shouts at me to watch *The*

Great British Bake Off. No, this one is really good! I am not so easily convinced.

Conventional psychological wisdom says that young brains in the first few years of life are at their most vulnerable and impressionable. But the twenties, at least in privileged middle-class US culture, still most certainly constitutes a time of teetering. Will I be this kind of person or that kind? The kind who wants to find purpose in her work or wants to make money? Get married or have adventures? And other mutually exclusive choices. I didn't pay much meta attention to these TV events I described above; I just consumed them like millions of others. So maybe the way a child who grows up in a house full of people yelling all the time feels more secure and cozy around loud people later in life but is completely unaware of this tendency, I developed an under-the-surface predilection for over-the-top media events. It took a while to get through to the gray matter and a level of consciousness about what I—what *we*—were watching.

But perhaps unlike the child who never quite understands his penchant for shouters until at least a year into therapy, there was one clear moment when I started to really think about TV as a cultural force. It was in the Harvard Bookstore Café on Newbury Street in Boston one crowded and boisterous evening in the early 1990s. I overheard a guy at the next table talking with his friend about the *Brady Bunch* episode wherein Marcia falls in love with her new dentist. He was stumbling a bit in trying to recall the doctor's name. "Vogel," I offered, as unobtrusively as I could, unable to contain myself. "Dr. Vogel!" he hollered, triumphantly, and we and our twenty-something companions shared a warm round of laughter and camaraderie.

The sort of memory lapse that café guy had happens all the time. Someone wonders aloud trying to recall the name of, say, Toronto's crack-smoking mayor or Air Supply's 1983 hit single, and it used to be that a passerby could jump in with the answer. A lovely moment of we-are-all-one occurs. Now there is no need for human interaction. Our phones know all. But that moment in the Harvard Bookstore Café took hold of me and meant way more than it had any right to. I was taken by the fact that we were relative adults remembering a show that, while surely in syndication somewhere, had been off the air for twenty years; the fact that I was attuned to this stranger's conversation certainly by key words either Marcia or Brady; that he found the episode worthy of talking about for whatever reason—perhaps he was weighing the pros and cons of his own May-December relationship or had started seeing a new hot dentist; that he happened to be within shoulder-brushing distance of a fellow pop culture traveler of a certain age who knew of what he spoke. I found it galvanizing and profound that a TV show brought us together for a brief, cheerful moment of shared experience that required no exposition. Remember me harping on "people watching the same thing at the same time" earlier? This was also the genesis of my fascination with generational characteristics. The TV version montage of my awakening would have me spotting and then hastily purchasing a copy of the newly published *Generation X* by Douglas Coupland on my way out of the bookstore that very night. While I understood all the factors that Coupland—and countless others—provided to explain what constitutes a generation's personality (though this concept is also roundly criticized as ridiculously simplistic and fatuous), it will be a cold day in hell before anyone convinces me that TV is not the most salient of those defining factors.

But I was not then the type of person to whom it would occur that this newfound interest signaled, finally, something to do with my life. It's clear to me now that a savvier more self-aware person, perhaps one who grew up in a house full of academics or who went to a progressive, interdisciplinary studies-oriented university, would have immediately begun researching doctoral programs in communications or media studies, or at least sociology or cultural studies, or someplace other than where I channeled it.

My first truly professional job was at an institution of higher education in Cambridge, Massachusetts. No, not that one. It was the very college that granted me my first of too many master's degrees, this one in counseling psychology. I had no idea what an idyllic employment situation I had until long after I left. Even though I worked with a bunch of psychotherapists, they were the sanest and most genuine bunch of people I've ever known, let alone had the privilege to work with. My job entailed liaising with several other administrative offices outside our department, and I was equally fortunate to find in these colleagues a group of people with similar tastes and quirks. One of our mainstay common pleasures was pop culture, specifically TV, specifically *Beverly Hills, 90210* and *Melrose Place*. All of us were somewhere in our late twenties at the time, a bit too old to be enjoying those Aaron Spelling candy-coated melodramas with such unabashed gusto, but there we were. (Around the same time, I was rushing home from an evening class to catch the yuppie opening sequence of *Thirtysomething*, a concurrent show that was also not strictly "for" me, though at twenty-eight I assumed that I was on the cusp of embracing a comfortable, affluent lifestyle surrounded by longtime self-centered and complicated friends. Where was the show for my inner Goldilocks?) We had lunch together daily and talked trash about Brenda, Brandon, Donna, Kelly, Dylan (and sometimes

Andrea), until after months of this we decided we should document our brilliant musings. Nothing had me learning the ins and outs of Microsoft Word faster than creating columns and centering a title and formatting a page. I granted myself the title of production editor. We had five staff writers including me, as well as occasional guest contributors. We (the world?) didn't have email yet, so I became skilled at using the department copy machine at low-traffic times and clearing paper jams in a jiffy. We distributed the product on foot by hand to the campus readership (I think we reached a circulation of fifteen). Though we generally watched the shows separately in our homes (like proper TV critics), we did assemble to watch one season finale during which the cable went out, and the keening coming from Joe's apartment during that horrific two seconds caused neighborhood dogs to join in the woeful chorus.

This cohort also spent a good deal of time discussing the Tonya Harding and Nancy Kerrigan scandal of 1994—sure, I mean the one that arose during the Olympics, but we didn't associate their tussle with the actual Games—organically representing a microcosm of the class warfare waging across the land. I was on Team Tonya, acting out my suppressed feelings of hostility and resentment toward my childhood friends who were entitled to Girl Scouts instead of Campfire Girls and Levi's red tag backpacks vs. off-brand orange tag and dancing school instead of no dancing school. We took sides with paper dolls we fashioned out of magazine images glued onto plastic knives and jammed into Styrofoam cup bases, reenacting the ghastly scenes—the broken skate lace and the "Why? Why? Why?" that we saw on a reel on every news and entertainment program for months. Our feelings about this current event worked their way into the *90210* newsletter (an opportunity for significant coverage of Andrea finally presented itself, she being the one who had to fake her address to go to the "good" high school instead of the Van Nuys one she was zoned for).

I was in a writing group with a few women friends at the same time, where I composed contrived and sappy short stories about couples who couldn't make it work despite their love. But these stories read like someone trying to be a writer. The *90210* newsletter was an outlet for self-expression and, as it turned out, one that suited my character perfectly. When I went into the *90210* archives after nearly a decade, I was astounded by our dedication and was envious of my own youth. We were nasty and dishy, high on our own perceived razor wits. I wrote in my true voice, like I talked, for the most part. (I don't know whether to be gratified or mortified that my style has changed little in a quarter century). We weren't the *Harvard Lampoon* or *Spy Magazine*, nor did we have much if any awareness of these entities or the legacy of literary satire. Just as the artisanal celebrity stalking of my tween years seemed to live in a vacuum, so this felt like something we invented together. But as snark purveyors as well as genuine fans, dare I say we were doing what loads of people are doing now on TV (aftershows like *Talking Dead*, *Talking Bad*, *Talking Saul*, and *Thronecast*) and on the internet (fully 95 percent of blogs in existence devote ample space to TV talk). And like any ambitious creatives, we capitalized on our modest success and took our venture to another level. We put on a show. We wrote and performed a skit at a celebration centered on some college milestone, via *90210* characters. It's documented on a VHS that I have in the archives but which will soon require special antique equipment to view, if it doesn't disintegrate when I take it out of the box.

Just as I didn't fully appreciate that great job I had, I also didn't realize that I would never again have this kind of camaraderie at a workplace, not to mention the freedom to indulge it. We were one another's touchstone, news source, sounding board, audience. Everything that happened was discussed and turned into a joke (Kurt Cobain's suicide a notable exception). We were social media in vivo. This educational institution, literally in Harvard's shadow, was fertile ground for my pop culture passion. I suppose it could be that I simply gravitated toward people with like interests, but it seemed for all the world like the entire leafy campus was the center of the zeitgeist and that anyone setting foot there was a part of the dishy, sassy, celebrity-obsessed vortex. In reality, there was all sorts of learning going on, and certainly some interesting research in education (Matt Damon's mother, Nancy Carlsson-Paige, was a faculty member there and a pioneer in peaceable classrooms and the effects of war toys on children). I had gotten my own degree from the place, so I knew there were excellent faculty doing things to help people. But as I gradually lost whatever desire had propelled me toward the human service professions, I let myself wander down a path of zero resistance. *90210* was my gateway, but soon enough, I was introduced to a stronger drug by two wicked temptresses from the admissions office (who also introduced me to MAC cosmetics, which meant buying expensive lipstick that made my lips look no different). This was the LSD trip known as *Absolutely Fabulous*.

Laura, my cool Cobain-worshipping sister from the *90210* editorial team (she named her first child Kurt), Jennifer, and I would take a VHS tape to my nearby apartment during our lunch break and could squeeze in two episodes if we sacrificed the "Wheels on Fire" intro, feeling hedonistic and entitled, inspired by our heroines, Patsy and Edina. At first I had a rough go of understanding their accents, but with an immersion program of twelve episodes in a month, I became confidently fluent in Holland Park English. That was also my entrée to the world of British comedy. I am fully aware that claiming *Fawlty Towers* or *Monty Python* as the source would give me more comedy cred, but it just wasn't the case. The brash display of shallowness and selfishness (e.g., "You cannot give these sorts of clothes to the poor! Darling, I'm sure they've got enough to contend with without the added humiliation of wearing last season's, sweetie!"; "You wouldn't have that birthday if I hadn't been generous enough to uncross my legs and give you to the world, darling. Nobody's thanked me, have they?"; "The last mosquito that bit me had to check into the Betty Ford clinic") was so liberating and exhilarating, I didn't think I could ever return to American network TV.

But my tastes were elastic, as they always had been. There was Must See TV, that arrogant slogan, but actually, yes, I did have to see the Thursday night lineup of *Friends*, *Mad About You*, and *Seinfeld*. Compared to *Ab Fab* they were tame, but they were clever, and because they more accurately mirrored my demographic (albeit outrageously exaggerated employment- and apartment-wise), I was compelled to indulge. Did I have the Rachel haircut, you wonder? I had the Dorothy Hamill almost two decades earlier, so yes, it follows suit that I would succumb to yet another hairstyle proffered by television that had no business near my hair's personality. Thanks to my friend Paul, another workmate with a penchant for the irreligious, I was invited into the world of the Canadian comedy crew of *Kids in the Hall*, rounding out my international English-language fare.

I can't gloss over that tired trope of complaining about how Monica and Rachel's apartment on the corner of Grove and Bedford in no way reflects the reality of the salaries of a chef and whatever Rachel was. But it is an inescapable fact that as an adult I pay far more attention to people's fictional TV living situations than I did when I was a kid who took real estate for granted because I didn't have to pay for it. (*Seinfeld*, with his bike hanging from the ceiling outside his bathroom, is much more true to NYC life, though Jerry was the last person you'd expect to see getting on a bike.) Many of the TV sitcoms that aired during my young, blissfully mortgage- and rent-free days were set in the suburbs. I knew suburban life because I had lived in it. I went to a classic brick TV-worthy high school with wide front steps and a clock tower. I walked to it down tree-lined sidewalks bordered by actual berms and lawns sprouting danger signs about alarm systems and fertilizer that could harm your kids or pets if they dared to trespass upon it. I saw my family's general standard of living reflected in shows like *Roseanne* and *The Wonder Years* and gradually taking on the trappings of *Eight Is Enough*, whose symmetrical Georgian facade was a larger version of the one we bought from the M family. We had a guest bedroom, a place where you could leave the ironing board set up and that you could avoid heating in the winter by closing the door, fooling the house into thinking it was smaller. I also saw fancy houses and lifestyles like those of the Bradys and the Cosbys, in their spacious living rooms where people stood around unnaturally, miles from bumping their shins on a coffee table, but I never felt an ounce of envy. They seemed unrealistic and lacking in what I considered to be charm, and I was too innocent to entertain ideas of economic disparity or the unrelenting requirement of earning an income myself.

The homes and lives that I remember most fondly took place in modest, urban apartments—*I Love Lucy*, *That Girl*, *Rhoda*. Even *All in the Family*'s 704 Hauser Street, though a misleadingly roomy and uncluttered house with an upstairs and a porch, seemed cozy and pleasing, somehow signaling the urban air in which it was situated as it shifted and groaned with age and working-class strain year by year. I suppose some people looked at TV and fantasized about a roomy *Brady*-like living space, or perhaps theirs was already like that or they assumed their own adult house would have one, but I envied Gabe and Julie Kotter and their tiny dollhouse-sized kitchen, where Julie could take the tuna casserole from the oven and put it on the minuscule dining table without having to take any steps; and MTM's sunken living room with bookshelves and floor-to-ceiling windows looking out over the Minneapolis winter trees. *One Day at a Time* took place in Indianapolis, but it barely mattered. They had a cool apartment and a super. On *Good Times*, Willona and little Janet Jackson popped over without having to put their coats on. Though I wasn't consciously assessing the homes of my TV characters, my predilection for cramped quarters may have something to do with my penchant for cities. I, too, can transport dinner from stove to dining table without lifting my feet, so I am, essentially, living my dream.

The city dwellers had more interesting jobs, or at least jobs that I could comprehend. Archie worked at a loading dock. That was physical labor, like the kind my dad did while he was going to night school, working in the plant of a metal products manufacturer where I would visit and wade through the sharp curlicue shavings and pocket little remnants of scrap to furnish my dollhouse. Gabe was a teacher. Alice was a waitress. Bob was a psychologist. Monica a chef. Of course people had graspable jobs in the suburbs and minor cities, too—Major Nelson was an astronaut; Darrin Stephens was an ad man—but as a rule, the typical sitcom dad had the typical dad job. Jim Anderson was an insurance agent providing for his family in Springfield, Midwest USA, establishing the idealized American family model, followed in short order by another pipe-and-slippers dad, Ward Cleaver. Kevin Arnold's dad, in his prime working years during the Vietnam War and revolutionary late 1960s, was in middle management for a defense contractor. None of their wives had jobs outside their tidy homes.

Plenty of women, usually single, had jobs that I basically understood. Mary Richards and Murphy Brown worked in TV news. Jamie Lee Curtis worked at a magazine with Richard Lewis in *Anything But Love*, Maura Tierney worked with Dave Foley at an AM station in *News Radio*. They lived in Minneapolis, Washington, Chicago, and New York. They had wry coworkers. Here is where the old me would veer off into the scholarly research and look for media scholars who have deconstructed the portrayal of work on TV from the 1950s to the present (of which there is a bounty), but no, I am not going there. Because that doesn't matter. What matters is my experience and yours. And my suggestion that maybe, just maybe, these shows had some tiny little nudging impact on where we ended up living and working. Suburbs, in my estimation, were the setting for too-big houses and formless jobs and dull coworkers. Cities were sassy and colorful. If you're wondering why I haven't given more space to *Ally McBeal*, a single lawyer in Boston with wisecracking male colleagues progressively using the same bathroom, it's because I only watched some of it, and it doesn't fit into my neat career choice theory except that Ally, like me, moved from Boston to NYC.

The genre of workplace comedies was where I likely began to imagine how my adult life might look. As an only child, I didn't have a set of characters on TV who looked like me. Did you ever notice that adult TV characters rarely mention siblings unless they are also characters on the show but that child characters are rarely singletons? It's all part of the what-makes-good-television code. Families with multiple children are fertile fields for conflict and/or humor—not so for only children. I did find some emotional solidarity with Jan Brady, whose middle-sibling status had a similar no-one-understands-me element. And writers probably don't want to muck up an adult character's backstory with a pointless sibling. I know not all siblings go at it like boxers in the ring, but I didn't have the learning lab to give it and take it, like Becky and Darlene or Bud and Kelly or even Niles and Fraser. So maybe my chance to rib and get ribbed by my peers good-naturedly but also cruelly would come later, I may have subconsciously been thinking, when I had a job. The way Frank and Hawkeye, Hank and Larry Sanders, the *WKRP* staff and the *Barney Miller* and *Murphy Brown* teams went at it at work—that was appealing to me. I did have one job where I felt we could have televised our repartee (in fact we did record it, see above), but other than that, I often felt like a fish out of water, maybe just one office building away from where my tribe was. Even now, I find myself saving up one-liners or clever turns of phrase that I'll unleash in a meeting or at the water bubbler, but who am I imagining to be my audience? Liz Lemon and Selina Meyer? My real-life coworkers are smart and kind and generally exhibit decorum, and if anyone is going to let a cynical, off-color joke fly, it's me, so I'm not really going to impress anyone.

The same month that we, the viewers, glommed onto the Olympic whack heard 'round the world, I got myself a cat. I didn't have a name chosen before I met her, and she didn't inspire an obvious one right away, so I looked around my apartment and alit upon the latest issue of *Vanity Fair* lying on a chair with Roseanne (then Arnold) on the cover. She was sporting a black lace teddy and straddling a chair. Nothing kittenish about her, but I had landed on the right thing. *Roseanne* was in the upper middle of its nine-year run, and I was a devoted fan. Rosie the cat never went by her full name, and her outward personality really could not have been more different from the real Roseanne's, but Rosie the cat and I shared a sarcastic sense of humor and the inability to suffer fools. Within a year, we moved to New York, to make all our dreams come true.

9

Big City of Dreams

The 1980s, for me, had included the end of high school, all of college, and the start of my adult life. Probably more change occurred from *Bosom Buddies* in 1980 to the first episode of the first *Real World* in 1992 than any other period of my life. On paper that is true, and in retrospect I suppose I grew up in many ways, but I don't feel like I really closed the parentheses of adolescence until I moved to New York City at age thirty.

Encountering the internet for the first time, in 1996, I may have gotten some inkling of the dizzying, altered state that people felt fifty years earlier when they first saw television. As soon as I had access to this mysterious universe of the World Wide Web, via a twelve-pound laptop and screeching modem that took about eighteen hours to hook up and configure (where that sound itself was once thrilling and *Jetsons*-like, now it's Flintstonian). I tried out this odd thing I kept seeing on Comedy Central while watching *Ab Fab*, encouraging me to go to comedycentral.com (what is that lack of spacing and odd punctuation communicating?) and type in AOL keyword: AbFab. I could not get my head around what any of it meant (in essence they were proto hashtags, which later gave me the same head-scratchy feeling; so many symbols! How does one read much less pronounce those messy things?), but when the blinking green underscore on my computer's screen seemed to prompt me to do so, I typed in the required text. Suddenly I had broken some kind of time/space barrier and was inside, sifting through a flow of green text on a black background providing an episode guide, a schedule, and merch descriptions. I was giddy, feeling like I had been granted entrance to a secret world no longer beholden to the laws of physics. That was just the appetizer. At the NYU journalism department, the real computers allowed me to see the images, and my brains fell out of my head. In reporting class when I was supposed to be looking up news articles on micro-local zoning regulations, I was investigating my new fandom portal. It was so simplistic and pointless, really, but it was the same with Pong, the rudimentary video game that came into my life in 1977 (we had the Digitek 2001, that super-sleek boomerang console that had tennis, hockey, squash, and "practice"), and that didn't stop me from playing for three hours at a stretch (against myself). That was a mere hint of where I would find myself in 1996—at the entrance to the rabbit hole.

Rewind a couple of years. In 1994 we were just starting to get desktop computers in dribs and drabs at that non-Harvard institution where I was employed. When I got mine, I had no idea what to use it for. As an academic advisor, I was able to log into some system that granted me the power to tell students what courses still had seats left, even if they weren't ones they really wanted to take. Other than saving a student a trip to the registrar's office and getting the bad news there, it was not an enormous added value. But I found a use for the word processing program in short order. It's possible the *90210* newsletter would not have come to fruition without it, given that I didn't have a typewriter. (I cannot imagine what was on my desk pre-1994 other than some Post-it Note pads and a coffee-stained blotter that predated my arrival.) So this is a case which some might love to seize as technology driving creativity. I like to think it would have happened even if we'd had only a letterpress (which would be so cool now!). That's how driven we were to create, express, and impress. The computer did drive something else unexpected, however. Melinda, one of my newsletter conspirators and fellow Tonya Harding advocate, and, not incidentally, the same friend who emailed me about the death of Mary Tyler Moore over twenty years later, printed out something for me that she had seen on a listserv (a word that made no sense and seemed misspelled). She couldn't forward it to me, as we had no email (a concept that made no sense and seemed to be missing letters). But somehow, Melinda was on technology's cutting edge and already belonged to some online group (a what, now?). The little snippet she espied was the announcement of a new concentration in cultural reporting and criticism in New York University's graduate journalism program (henceforth, CRC). Melinda thought it seemed up my alley. If I couldn't recognize my own leanings, at least someone else could. Things began to come into focus.

I already had a graduate degree—a master's in counseling psychology from the very program for which I was then advising other students and stealing company time to pen a pop culture zine—which I wasn't using for its intended purpose, though I cannot deny that it had served me well up to that point. I quickly decided to apply and let fate take its course. A few months later I was driving a one-way rental car to my new apartment in Brooklyn, Rosie the cat in a carrier in the passenger seat, and most of my earthly possessions squished into every other part of the car. I was thirty years old and felt all at once like a wise traveler and someone who had just graduated from middle school—I was exactly that anxious, naive, and cocky. What about the drug pushers in New York??

Ellen Willis (I promised she'd be back), the creator of the brand-new CRC, gathered her disciples together in an awkward sit-and-meet where we introduced ourselves in turn by identifying our areas of interest. I remember a few music people, lots of art people, a couple of film people—just what you'd expect. Two women stood out to me because of their quirkier sounding plans—one was "textiles." The other—get a load of this—was "food." (While it's nearly impossible to imagine a time when we of the Western Hemisphere were not smitten by this topic and considering ourselves all experts ridiculously labeling ourselves with the pathetic, infantilizing "foodie," in 1995 it was a newspaper beat still relegated to a corner of the style section. The Food Network was only two years old, so we really knew only Emeril and Sara Moulton.) Well, it takes all kinds, I thought, impressed by their clear-headed if eccentric directions. As we went around, I was an outlier, too, as the only person who claimed television. Ellen was immediately supportive. "We need more good writing about television," she said, as adamantly as she could muster. While I was already committed to my area, her words carried me through some doubtful times over the next year and half (plus twenty-five more). All three of us weirdos—myself, Alison (textiles), and Megan (food)—have remained good friends, and two of us have made a decent living off of our original topics (hint: not me, unless ten million of you bought this book).

I was able to feed my TV starter dough fairly regularly, thanks to the few classes we had that defined us as the CRC-ers.

In some of them, the assigned readings were actually exclusively about TV. They were included in course packets I marked up neatly and heavily—some of my notes indicate that I used to be smarter than I am now, at least for a while—and have survived the several moves I've made around New York over the last twenty-plus years. There was a fair-use-violating volume of photocopied excerpts from Martin Williams's *TV: The Casual Art*, which I consumed like a starving dog. I also hungrily scavenged for pro-TV arguments in adjacent cultural tracts like Walter Benjamin's "The Work of Art in the Age of Mechanical Reproduction," Gilbert Seldes's *The Seven Lively Arts*, and Susan Sontag's "Notes on Camp." Just about any of the new journalists inspired me with their gonzo methods and unconventional style. I like to think that Tom Wolfe, for example, wouldn't be so hypocritical as to scoff at TV when he covered subjects like kustom kars and Merry Pranksters, even though I suspect many of them would deem TV to be a stodgy tool of mainstream culture and worthy more of disdain than critical analysis. Sontag reportedly thought of TV as "cultural drivel" and "the end of Western civilization," but she had other positive attributes.

As a member of the inaugural CRC group, we were the beneficiaries of side-eye from some of the faculty and the hard-news students, not unlike a bunch of longhairs infiltrating a Model UN meeting, though our cultural gap was better exemplified by Woodward and Bernstein wannabes vs. Gay Talese and Joan Didion acolytes. We were forced to mingle in the basic classes, but we CRC-ers found refuge in our ghetto, reading McLuhan, bell hooks, Pauline Kael, and Dwight MacDonald and talking in extremely serious—often heated—tones about Pearl Jam and Beavis and Butt-Head. I was completely ill equipped and physically ill at ease as a fake cub reporter at city hall press conferences and collecting man on the street interviews at the West

Village Halloween parade, and while I was forced to confront my chasm of cultural literacy in the CRC classes, at least I was among compatriots.

I can only imagine the infighting that went on in the presumed years it must have taken for Ellen to get her program approved and off the ground. The faculty was (it is quite different now, more modernized and inclusive) dominated by hard-boiled, mostly white male, journalists. One day I'd be in a class being quizzed on headlines on page B3 of that morning's *New York Times* (we were told in no uncertain terms that you cannot hope to be an even adequate journalist if you don't read the Paper of Record cover to cover on a daily basis). The next day, I'd be instigating an invigorating argument with my professor—me, the consummate student wallflower for all my school-age years—about the prosocial value of *Roseanne*. It was created by real people with real issues! It's based on real life! These days so much is made of the pedagogical and emotional intelligence developed by reading fiction. So why couldn't he and all the other TV naysayers see that same value in *watching* fiction? We're told not to judge what people are reading—again, these days, so perhaps this is because video killed not only the radio star but also the printed word—but just to rejoice in the fact of their reading at all, right? I'll tell you why. The televised—not the visual, because film is usually given the same level of respect as literary fiction—is prejudged to be empty calories, in a poorly veiled display of class bias.

There were cultural gulfs within the CRC posse, too, to be sure—the ones who focused on hip-hop or the downtown art scene or dance, for instance, were edgier or grittier and therefore more "relevant" by some unspoken standard of New York cool—but what we had in common was our relative outsider status within the journalism program, and we reveled in it.

Some of the students were drawn to the program specifically because of Ellen and, as such, fancied themselves rebels and "born in the wrong decade." Others of us were merely relieved to have found a place that took our interests seriously.

I wrote my first published TV piece for a short-lived newspaper funded by open air garage magnate Al Hirschfield (not to be confused with celebrity caricaturist, the Line King, Al Hirschfeld), called *Open Air PM*. My subject was a review of the premiere of *The Daily Show*, whose first host was Craig Kilborn. In my fifth-floor West Village walkup, I still had no cable (ergo, no Comedy Central of my own) and still didn't know how to steal it, so I watched it at Ellen's apartment on a regular-sized, color TV while I was house sitting for her. She and her family had no pets, but every inch of wall space was lined floor to ceiling with books, and perhaps that is what I was keeping watch over. I concluded, ever so prophetically, that this *Daily Show* thing showed promise, that it was a "fairly satisfying satire whose mockery radiates in multiple directions." My full-page article looked so fancy (*Open Air*'s format was sophisticated, and they were big into images as the centerpiece), and I was sure I was on my way to continued absolute fabulousity as a TV critic, probably a regular column. I wrote a few other pieces for their "Open Tube" section—reviews of Rosie O'Donnell's talk show, another Manhattan-based journalism industry sitcom called *Ink*, starring Mary Steenburgen and Ted Danson, and an Aaron Spelling series called *7th Heaven*, whose first paragraph was one sentence that read, "I miss *Melrose*." For the NYU student rag, *Washington Square News*, I reviewed *Boston Common*, a sitcom starring comedian Anthony Clark; *Saturday Night Special*, a six-episode late-night sketch show hosted by Roseanne and rife with A-list guests; *Good Company*, a one-season NYC-based workplace sitcom starring Wendie

Malick. I even did a phone interview with Andrew Dice Clay. I was terrified and he sensed it and was impatient and unpleasant and not in a shticky way. But suddenly I was a celebrity journalist! My dream of a successful career in New York City was on the cusp of coming true in less than a year. *What's this about journalism or NYC being hard to break into?* I wondered idiotically as I perused the *Village Voice* for apartments soon not to be out of my price range. I can now make it anywhere! I will get my sunken living room yet!

Fast-forward a decade where I had added approximately zero bylines to the world, with the exception of a small pile of printouts of TV show synopses for an early *New York Times* digital offshoot called *New York Today* and was fact-checking "Great Grilling Recipes" and "How Stress Makes You Fat" at *Ladies' Home Journal*. A decade-long career in editorial research at women's magazines had proven a more practical route to making a steady living than my attempts at freelance writing. My journalism school education did provide me with the solid grounding for the "reverse reporting" techniques of fact checking, even though no faculty advisor would dare mention it as a career path option. I would later refer to my NYU knowledge—especially the CRC parts—when I stumbled into different kinds of writing opportunities, so stay tuned. Props to J-school for giving me the space to finally focus on what I thought about TV and what other people thought about TV (and art, culture, and criticism).

Most of the essays we read that were explicitly about TV were demonizing screeds. As soon as I had landed on the shores of the new world of NYC, I found myself feeling vindicated in my new serious TV career one minute, and ham-handedly or apoplectically (depending on my audience) defending it the next. And this was all within one building in the vast lower

Manhattan domain lorded over by NYU. In contrast to the paeans to TV that I mentioned a moment ago, I was also forced to acknowledge the arguments of the likes of anti-TV advocates Newton Minow, Jerry Mander, Mark Crispin Miller, Neil Postman, and the family values crusaders. Neil Postman, an eminent professor and scholar in NYU's Department of Media, Culture and Communication, was the speaker at a brown bag lunch in the journalism department one afternoon, and I don't think we hissed, but a couple of my fellow CRC-ers and I thought about it, because we regarded him and his ilk as the enemy. We were staking our careers on the importance and meaning of popular culture and entertainment in all its forms, and this guy was dissing it, saying that entertainment obscured meaningful public discourse. We felt so intellectual in our silent protest. Now, twenty-five years later, I have to contend with my earlier fist-in-the-air self and see Postman's arguments for what they are and realize—in large part thanks to the many Postman-esque feelings I now have about the internet—that I agree with him more than I used to. We may indeed be digitally amusing ourselves to death. But I'll come back to my verdict on this later.

10

Good vs. Bad

Time marches on, brains age, cultures supposedly evolve, and the detractor-advocate helix exists evermore. I have said aloud on numerous occasions that the internet has ruined my attention span and made me lazier and stupider. I am sure this is what my middle-aged counterparts said of TV in the first couple decades of its cultural domination. That statement I made earlier about the internet being wonderful and horrible? Not only did I not invent that thought, but Neil Postman himself was fond of saying, way before the internet, that technological change always results in winners and losers. It was true of television, too. In fact, lots of things in the universe are wonderful and horrible, winners and losers, many of which we interact with on a daily basis. Two examples that spring to mind: food and people. The job for us, then, is to assess on a case-by-case basis the manifestations or iterations with which we come in contact. I could be wrong, but my sense is that a lot of anti-TV dogmatists wrote off the whole enterprise a) off the bat because they didn't like one show; b) because they didn't like the concept and never watched any show; or c) to get attention. I made an analogy earlier—grocery store is to "junk food building" as television is to "idiot box"—to make the point that it's unfair to tar a whole medium with the same critical brush, and I reiterate it here with emphasis because there are so very many different aisles and products to choose from in TV nowadays. Once we judge a cultural product, what do we do with it? Condemn it? Consume it? Condemn and consume in either order?

By the way, these anti-TV curmudgeons would all unwittingly back me up in my "TV matters" argument. If it didn't matter, they wouldn't be getting their starchy undergarments in such a bunch about it. Writing it off, being one of those people who says, "I don't watch TV," with a dismissive air, is not an appealing quality, unless you're a single person seeking a mate at a family-values or "high-level" academic conference. It's a copout. One of my favorite writers, the late Jenny Diski, said it more eloquently: "We are what we are. It's not possible (or attractive) to be better than we are simply by morally withdrawing from the mess." She was referring, among other supposed bad habits, to eating meat and smoking. She didn't want to stop smoking, she said, in part because she didn't want to be one of those smug ex-smokers. Nobody likes a smug person. I don't know how else to tell you. But I don't have to tell you. You're reading this book. The others would probably just snort if they saw my book in the store, library, or internet and move on. They wouldn't even be curious enough to open their minds and wonder, What does she love about TV so much? And that's the difference between those close-minded, staid critics and people like us, readers and writer of this book. We'll watch anything—*Masterpiece Theatre* and *Growing Up Kardashian* (I know that seems like the laziest autofill for that idea, but it makes my point so clearly). And, I don't think I need to tell you, friends, that we're better for it.

These crusaders weren't just men and/or academics. There was and is an entity innocuously called the Media Research Center that came to my attention as a nascent TV expert when I discovered a little pamphlet they produced called *Family Guide to Prime Time Television*. I had the 1995–1996 edition of this gem, a thirty-six-page booklet listing all the prime-time network programs with a little traffic light symbol next to each indicating green, yellow, or red. It was put together by the Parents Television Council as a special project of the Media Research Center, which turned out to be a conservative watchdog group whose "sole mission is to expose and neutralize the propaganda arm of the Left: the national news media."

I imagine Anita Bryant, Phyllis Schlafly and a bunch of on-board parents sitting at card tables in the fluorescently lit gymnasium of a parochial school, the kind that always smells like lemon floor cleaner and hypocrisy, sternly curating this opus. But given that the back of the pamphlet gives credit to former US education secretary Bill Bennett, Shirley Jones, and Dee Wallace Stone (E.T.'s unwitting host mom), it probably took place in a glass-and-steel Los Angeles high-rise. To provide a flavor of the rating system, here are excerpts from the case briefs for some of my favorite shows of the period:

> *Roseanne*: " . . . Roseanne stars as a member of a somewhat dysfunctional extended family. . . . *Roseanne* has showcased foul language ('ass,' 'suck'), condoned premarital sex and disrespect for parental authority, and addressed adult-oriented subject matter such as homosexuality. According to press reports, *Roseanne* will host a gay wedding on a future installment." (Red light)

> *Seinfeld*: " . . . the show almost completely avoids social commentary. Nonetheless, sex is *Seinfeld*'s favorite subject matter,

and the four main characters spend a great deal of time talking about it, pursuing it, and having it, albeit off-camera. While the series is not at all explicit, it can be extremely suggestive, and has centered episodes on masturbation, oral sex, and homosexuality. Moreover, Seinfeld never suggests that this conduct is morally objectionable or offensive." (Red light)

Beverly Hills, 90210: "While extramarital sex is shown to have devastating effects, main characters regularly engage in premarital sex, and have yet to face any negative consequences. . . . The brightest note: a regular who vows to remain a virgin until her wedding night." (Red light)

Friends: " . . . endorsed lesbian parenting." (Red light)

Ellen: "*Ellen* frequently introduces sex as a main topic of conversation among the characters. Premarital sex and adultery are treated casually." (Somehow she skated by with a yellow, though a couple of years later would have earned a red and, if it were possible, an earsplitting siren.)

Green-lit programs involved the vague term "family-friendly themes," rather than listing explicit family-friendly activities, and "respect for parental authority" seems to be a highly prized characteristic.

These supposed accusations hardly merit comment, but I can't resist a few. The Conner family was likely far more functional than many if not most of those families who were reading the pamphlet in earnest. Many if not most people spend a great deal of time talking about sex, pursuing it, and having it, albeit off-camera. And Donna lost her virginity, unmarried, on college graduation night. Already I am guilty of giving too much ink to a group that believes homosexuality to be morally objectionable or offensive. Though I can say two positive things about this product: a) it's useful for families upholding conservative Christian values who want to shelter their children from reality and art, and b) it's a really handy size.

I can't stress enough how jarring it was for me to learn about the small but passionate army of people who thought so poorly of TV. It was not my first exposure to these types of groups, people who get so worked up about a thing that other people are doing that they could easily just ignore because they're not being affected by it (methinks they were the same group). It was not even the first time I was exposed to people so adamant about the evils of certain types of entertainment (to wit, Tipper Gore). All this control was so antithetical to how I was brought up. Not only did my parents not care or worry about what I was watching, they frequently enjoyed it with me. I cannot fathom having been squelched by a V-chip or hemmed in by a laundry list of no-no shows. I honestly don't know who I would be if I hadn't watched all that TV. And who I am is not a morally bereft person, though as an atheist and someone who had sexual relations outside of marriage and who thinks that people who think homosexuality is deviant are themselves mentally damaged, I would be deemed a demon by some. And they could blame Mike Stivic and Ann Romano and George Carlin, but *censor* TV shows? You can watch this but not that? It's as wrongheaded and as intellectually and culturally harmful as banning books. How are babies supposed to develop an immune system if they don't crawl around on the floor with a diverse community of bacteria? Same idea.

And here's something rather curious. In 2018, in the midst of a culture wars redux, *New York Times* writer Wesley Morris wrote an article called "Should Art Be a Battleground for Social

Justice?" wherein, because it was in the air we were breathing, it didn't even need to be stated that the group that was up in arms this time around were not the conservative, family values crowd, but progressive-minded folks, sometimes referred to as social justice warriors. The values upheld by these arbiters involve awareness of the backstory and current behavior of the makers of cultural products, and the results have the potential to overshadow, overpower, or willfully erase the art itself. The effect is more marked than it would be without the existence of prestige TV culture that differentiates itself from regular TV in its auteur focus, a foregrounding of the values of the writer/producer/show runner. So you could say it's the price we—the artist and the audience—pay for good TV. The new makers are at greater professional risk than their predecessors.

We are in the middle of wondering if this should be the case. There's enough written about the debate to wrap around the earth several million times, so I'll keep it short here. If twenty-five years ago you told me that *Roseanne* would be rebooted but shortly thereafter killed off her own show because of a racist tweet, that the big mouth that jump-started Roseanne's career was ultimately her downfall, I would have laughed in your face. I'd be so distracted by the confusion surrounding the use of "tweet," then "reboot," that it would take me some time to get to the kernel of "What in the name of the devil are you talking about?" I bring this up to remind us that everything is cyclical, people are different and have different values, morality is subjective and fungible, and oh yes—TV matters. It's a strange time to talk about history and TV and nostalgia because of the revelations and revolutions that have been coming to the fore on a weekly basis as I write this. A few of the TV shows that I watched in their entirety (and in repeats) are being white-washed from TV history. I may have been born with the gene for the ability to separate the art from the artist or maybe just into a generation to whom that comes more naturally, but I want *Roseanne* and *Louie* and *The Cosby Show* to stay in the sitcom catalog forever.

Neil Postman, the NYU media scholar, died in 2003, a year that is after the internet invaded Earth but before social media took the Western world hostage. Wondering if he publicly commented on this new electronic chapter of our cultural lives, I Googled: what did neil postman think of the internet? Which is not using good keyword protocol like we urge our students to do, but of course, as our students prove when they argue and defend their methods, it works. The first result (another temptation we caution students about, but fine, I will just stop telling them anything) was something titled, "What Neil Postman Thinks about the Internet." This well-reasoned, thought-provoking, imaginary interview written by a media studies professor and former student of Postman led me to a 1990 speech given by Postman called "Informing Ourselves to Death," which really should be more well known because of its prescience, right down to inadvertently evoking the then six-year-old Mark Zuckerberg (and a host of others of his generation): "By becoming masters of this wondrous technology, they will acquire prestige and power and some will even become famous." Some of his words enraged me the way they did in 1995, like this: "But I maintain that all of this [information propagation] is a monumental and dangerous waste of human talent and energy. Imagine what might be accomplished if this talent and energy were turned to philosophy, to theology, to the arts, to imaginative literature or to education." Well, that just sounds like philosopher and scholar Allan Bloom, he of *The Closing of the American Mind*, a book I hate-read several times trying to sharpen my arguments against cultural elitism, to little success.

Other words from the Postman speech, I was disappointed to discover but adult enough to confess, made me feel shameful about my reliance on the internet. And other words just freaked me out and made me wonder if maybe he didn't really die in 2003 after all and was in fact sitting in a comfortable overstuffed chair in a coffee shop near NYU, observing the world from behind an actual book. Words like this: "Through the computer, the heralds say, we will make education better, religion better, politics better, our minds better—best of all, ourselves better. This is, of course, nonsense, and only the young or the ignorant or the foolish could believe it." Because before I read that I was going to argue in my head with him by asking, "Aren't you gratified that I was so readily able to revisit your teachings by using the computer like I just did? Would you have preferred I go back to a print version of one of your books and reread and think and apply?" But I know he would say, "Yes, that is exactly what I would prefer that you do." And I would respond with the living version of a blushing, eyes-downcast emoji indicating deep shame.

Damn you, Postman, you Cassandra! When just remembering him, before reading the 1990 speech, just knowing he didn't have pretty things to say about the internet, I was ready to argue, "Yes, but television didn't have the same widespread, world-changing impact that the internet and social media are having! You can't compare the two!" But to be honest, I know he would say that they are not two different things, really, that TV paved the way for the internet and made us complacent and primed us for replacing face-to-face conversation with superficial face-to-screen contact. The mediums—electronic communication devices—are along the same continuum. And then, like Alvy Singer, he would trot out Marshall McLuhan from the edge of the frame of my mental vision, who would say,

"I told you so, too." And now I can't help but further imagine McLuhan saying (while Postman and Alvy Singer and even Annie Hall nod along), "You know nothing of my work! How a person like you even dared to utter my name in your book about television is totally amazing." TV seems quaint and harmless. But it was the gateway, turning us into passive automatons. The magic-bullet theory of mass media has been debunked by many who say: a) stop demeaning audiences, they are not passive, idiotic victims, and b) stop being so dramatic, no one's dying. But it's difficult to argue with the evidence at hand.

I am dangerously veering off course here because it's so tempting to continue this fake conversation with Postman (who's a stand-in for anyone who sees the TV glass as mostly empty). Well-developed and serious arguments about the positive effects of television on a societal level do not belong to this memoir. But I am champing at the bit to know what Postman would have to say about the alleged impact of satirical news programming over the past couple of decades, especially given the value he placed on civil discourse. Again, I turn to Ken Jennings from *Planet Funny*, because he's so good at well-developed and serious arguments but in a fun way, which is his very own point here. In referring to the "John Oliver effect" via HBO's *Last Week Tonight*, Jennings writes that the comedian's commentaries:

> have changed the status quo where years of think pieces and direct-mail appeals have not. . . . When Oliver explained the issues surrounding net neutrality, viewers submitted forty-seven thousand new comments to the FCC, enough to crash its website. He did a segment on how badly large poultry companies treat their suppliers, and the next appropriations bill to pass the House of Representatives strengthened legal protections for chicken farmers. A month after Oliver complained

> about the bail bond system in America, New York mayor Bill de Blasio announced reforms to the city's bail procedures. None of these issues were drifting anywhere close to the top of the public mind before *Last Week Tonight*'s writers dressed them up in jokes.

While Jennings's point is that humor helps the medicine go down, my reason for placing these facts politely in front of Postman's face would be to say, "Look what TV and the internet hath also wrought." I can never know what Postman would say, so I'll just drop the mic in my imagined scene and walk away, while tossing over my shoulder, because I never know when to shut it, "You know, there are good germs and bad germs, and we can benefit from both."

I can't believe I went on so long about Neil Postman, let alone even mentioned Tipper Gore. But it's vital and necessary, like we always tell our students: You must look at both sides, not just write your persuasive essay by seeking out those who share your views. With that duty out of the way, I want to now turn to people who unequivocally share, if not activated, my views.

Early me did not distinguish between "good" and "bad" television, maybe only between entertaining and boring. I even liked what was over my head. Current me has little tolerance for *watching* what I consider to be "bad," and even though I just said a bunch of stuff about subjectivity and diversity of values, I feel strongly that I know empirically which is which. But somewhere between early me and current me, I learned to *appreciate* both. The bad is just as useful as the good for telling us about ourselves—really it might even be the more sensitive barometer. There are two TV people (there might be a more respectful and accurate word for us, but I don't mind this one even though it signals part of the problem with entertainment scholarship) who are my favorite resources for this good/bad debate and for so many other things about television. One is longtime critic David Bianculli who is the founder and editor of TVWorthWatching.com and teaches TV and film history to college students. You might know him because he's the TV critic for *Fresh Air* and subs for Terry Gross a lot. I met him first via his book *Teleliteracy: Taking TV Seriously*, which fittingly was my first primer shortly after I figured out I was a TV person. In that book he talks about McLuhan and the wasteland and how TV teaches and deserves respect. I met David in person when he did a talk at the Media Studies Center where I worked at the time (around 1997), and to me he was a celebrity, and I was correspondingly atwitter. I met him again when he curated a wondrous exhibit titled *Bianculli's Personal Theory of TV Evolution* at a gallery in Tribeca. I don't normally have a wealth of patience for looking at objects in a museum, but I could have spent a few more hours looking at the ones in this room, which included Rod Serling's typewriter, a 1946 TV, and Mister Rogers's cardigan and sneakers. (Similarly, when in Chicago I head to the utterly engrossing Museum of Broadcast Communications and will visit the world-class Art Institute only if there's time.)

At this same event, I got to meet another of my TV people heroes, Bob Thompson. Bob is to TV studies what Alfred Kinsey is to sex research. He is a role model for taking that square peg you love and smashing it through a less-than-forgiving round hole and turning out some cool shapes in the process. The serious and well-researched history of the evolution of TV studies won't be summarized here, but Bob (as you might remember being introduced at the start of the book as the founding director of the Bleier Center for Television and Popular Culture at Syracuse University) was one of the pioneers. To get an informative and entertaining synopsis of what Bob did for TV, please seek out a 1989 segment from *60 Minutes* on YouTube. Searching "60 minutes bob thompson love boat" (without the quotes, obviously) will get you there. In addition to a young Bob, graduate students in ties, and lots of oversized eyeglasses the last time they were hip, you'll see Morley Safer cantankerously asking Horace Newcomb (another trailblazing TV ambassador), "What on earth do we have to learn from watching *Gunsmoke*?"

Thompson's been answering this question for decades. At Bianculli's Tribeca gallery event, Thompson asked the audience, "Why do smart people watch stupid things?" This provocatively blunt question reminds me of an Emily Nussbaum review wherein, in the context of the HBO 2018 adaptation of Elena Ferrante's *My Brilliant Friend*, she asks, "What kind of art do intelligent people talk about? What do they binge on, late at night? Which art form is capable of the most originality, the greater depth, the wider influence—and which one makes you rich? . . . It's enough to make you crave a broader conversation, with respect for the strengths of each art, an interplay that's more than a simple hierarchy." In just a few words she neatly encapsulates the basis for taking TV seriously. She suggests or pines for a comp lit protocol that welcomes TV into the canonical fold with traditional literature; she asks my favorite id-revealing question, which is what would you consume if you couldn't tell anyone about it; she reminds us that art is also a business; she acknowledges that art (including TV) matters.

Thompson and Bianculli carried on, good-naturedly disagreeing about bad TV. Thompson insisted *The Love Boat* was good art and related a relevant story where he skipped a Western Civ class at the University of Chicago to watch *CHIPs*. Bianculli, the journalist, adamantly eschews the "bad" and prides himself on steering viewers toward the "good." This leads to a larger meditation on the difference between scholar and critic, though not mutually exclusive, and the evolution of TV studies which—let's say it together now—*do not belong to this memoir*. Thompson argued that TV is so ubiquitous that it cannot be ignored but we "fail to see the significance." Thanks to people like Bob and Horace Newcomb, there are scholars all over the *world* studying TV the way they study classical literature.

I didn't know about people like Bob Thompson and David Bianculli when I was writing for the *90210* newsletter or getting excited about the guy in the bookstore café evoking Marcia Brady or even in my cultural reporting program when I was getting into the headspace of realizing that writing about popular culture actually had a vaunted tradition. I had figured I would write about TV somehow, somewhere, with only vague notions of the available outlets for such work (remember, I am pre-internet human). To illustrate my ignorance, at one time, in the early 1990s, I actually believed that I came up with original idea of reviewing TV awards shows (though in my defense, if I had never seen such a thing, perhaps it needed some more hands). There was a vast continuum between our *90210* newsletter and, you know, the *New Yorker*, but I was not aware of any of it. Perhaps I knew that being a TV critic was a thing, but I couldn't name a TV critic. The first one I came across as I dipped my toe into the sea of glossy and matte media that used to fill up actual newsstands and magazine stores in NYC, was John Leonard, who, in addition to being a book and cultural critic for a variety of high-profile publications, was the TV critic for *New York* magazine in the mid-1990s. I latched onto that and recall announcing to anyone who inquired about my intentions now that I had a journalism degree, "I want to be a TV critic, like John Leonard, for example." I'd say that as if just randomly choosing him from the long list of names in my brain when at that moment there was really just the one. I wanted to write like Calvin Trillin and Susan Orlean and Joan Didion and the *Vogue* food critic Jeffrey Steingarten (all my new writer heroes)—about TV.

There are many different first steps one can take on the proverbial thousand-mile journey. One way you can find out about a career is to go to a fair in a gymnasium or hotel function room where a bunch of tables are personed by representatives from selected professions. It's like a cafeteria. Oh that looks good, you might say at the forest ranger or human resources management table. I'm not allergic to any of those ingredients, so okay, maybe I'll try that. Another way is to follow in the footsteps of a family member, which is either very complicated or very straightforward, but hardly ever anything in between. Another way is to be lost and feel like you'll never land on anything, but in the meantime, one or more of the things you're using to distract yourself from feeling lost and loserish turn out to be things in and of themselves (Etsy or Marc Maron's *WTF* podcast would not exist if this were not true). And then, only after caroming around in your own lonely weird box, do you find out about these other people who have been making a living at doing the thing you thought—not in a good way—was yours alone. It gives you a real shot of you-can-do-this-ism that is maybe all you need to look around your scattered life and go into the mental archives and collect all this stuff that seemed unconnected and unmeaningful and paste it together into a collage that doesn't look half bad and makes you want to add more. And then you can keep adding to it, like Richard Dreyfus with the mashed potatoes in *Close Encounters of the Third Kind* but without frightening your family. "Yeah, this means something," you might say, and cry a little bit. You may not make a living at it alone, but it can keep you alive while you work at your day job. The rest of this book is pretty much about how this third way was the path that finally sort of worked for me.

11

The Third Way

When I started my job as an academic librarian in 2007, I took a deep breath, knowing that like every other faculty member in every university everywhere, I had to publish or perish. I loved being a librarian, but I was not so interested in reading—much less producing—the literature of the field. Librarianship was a third-ish career for me, and I did not possess that eager young professional's inspiration. But I didn't think writing an article on *Arrested Development* or *Weeds*, strategically studded with terms like "hegemonic" and "postmodern," would cut it for tenure. I had to at least make some pretense that I was a serious librarian-professor. So, my first article was a compromise, yet a subject I came to organically.

For pure enjoyment, I was rewatching *All in the Family*. After the sixth season, I bumped up against the end of the episodes available to me online or on disc (there were three more seasons out there somewhere) and became genuinely interested in the conundrum facing TV scholars in such situations. Even though the archives of television programming go back only seventy years or so, it's not as if you can get your hands on everything.

There was a lot of erasing of tapes because broadcasters needed more space and didn't think recording over shows—*The Tonight Show* being a classic, tragic example—would upset anyone. It was just a TV show, for crying out loud. For a while no one did care. But later on, when some enlightened people began to realize that even the crappiest shows are an important part of our cultural heritage, it was devastating. It's hard for me to imagine someone in the moment not having a panic attack about destroying the only copy of something, even if it was something that seemed totally worthless. I mean, the Library of Congress at one point took up the archiving of tweets. The collective mind-set—facilitated by technology—has evolved, which is advantageous for the vast amounts of crap being generated.

Here's an aside right up front. Though there are many points of overlap between the journalism and library science fields (research and information being the saturated center of the Venn diagram), there is a big cultural difference that smacked me in the face during one library school class. The assignment was to create a "pathfinder," which we now call "research guide," which is really to regular people just a list of resources—books, articles, videos, archival sources, etc.—on a particular subject. Mine was on TV cooking shows, since I was then writing my book about said topic and had a jillion items to populate a pathfinder. We were asked to share these finished products with our classmates. Since my book was still a mere draft, far from being published and therefore still a pipe dream, I was protective of all the work I'd put into it and thought some of the loud, popular girls in my class (yes, we were adult women, but some insecurities die hard, and yes, there are loud and popular people in library school) seemed suspiciously like they would steal my pathfinder, see the brilliance of my idea, use the sources to write a book, and, because of their cool-girl literary connections, become best-selling and rich based on my fabulous idea. "Idea theft is real," one of my journalism school compatriots gravely agreed when I shared my anxiety with her. I privately told my library professor I would prefer not to share mine, and while he stared at me wide-eyed for what seemed like two minutes before responding in a kind way, he announced to the class during the next meeting that anyone who didn't feel comfortable sharing their work didn't have to. When I tell that story to librarians now, they look at me the same way passengers do as I'm driving while telling them I failed my driver's test six times. But I assure them that I was rehabilitated. My former, paranoid, self-protective journalist persona has been replaced by a free-love, open-access, sunshiny, share-alike librarian.

In typical academic fashion, I tried to generate some prepublication buzz about my forthcoming book by writing an article. I had never written anything scholarly before, but being congenitally sarcastic, I thought I'd try writing a parody of an academic treatise in summarizing the evolution of TV cooking shows. It was accepted by *FLOW*, an online journal produced at the University of Texas at Austin, which is one of the hotbeds of serious TV studies. But it was interpreted completely at face value, not tongue-in-cheek. So I realized then that my friend was right when, in order to quell my self-doubt about my ability to write like a scholar, he told me that academic writing is just imitating a style. That knowledge, along with the publication of *Watching What We Eat* and then my article on *All in the Family*, allowed me to feel more comfortable with the idea of turning my TV interest into a vehicle for tenure and promotion.

In typical academic fashion, again, I spun sequels from some finished pieces into new ones. There was the article about Dione Lucas, an early TV cooking show host eclipsed by Julia Child, that I titled "A Kitchen of One's Own," which

I did intentionally to suggest that I am well versed in classic Anglophone literature as well as pop culture. I then moved into slightly different territory, visiting the Edward R. Murrow papers at Tufts University to scrounge up details about a long-forgotten program called *Small World*. Just last month, someone from Germany contacted me about that 2012 article, because in it I had described an episode featuring Aldous Huxley, and this German fellow and the fellow members of the International Aldous Huxley Society had never heard of any television appearances by Huxley. I offered some vague suggestions about how to find the video—I had seen the episode in the fortress of the Paley Center—but really this anecdote is about how someone actually read the article.

These articles were, as it turned out, considered worthy scholarly output, though the job of imitation did require the adoption of an unnatural tone and vocabulary words that I had to look up repeatedly and the incorporation of a superficial understanding of the corpus of various scholars. But I did it. I won! It was as if I had eaten nothing but Pop-Tarts and Bugles for my entire life and then learned that *JAMA* published a groundbreaking longitudinal study proving that processed food is the key to a long, disease-free life. I'm aware I'm not the only person to turn their love of TV (or video games or French movies or rap music) into an academic career, and I did not have the difficult time that Bob Thompson did (thanks in large part to him), but I did feel lonely. I would attend pop culture conferences where freak flags mingled with theory heads and industry people—but mostly freak flags. The conferences tend to attract a large number of people with a passion for fantasy literature and graphic novels. The TV-specific panels usually number around one or two, where the number of panels with the word "zombies" in the title would at least quadruple that, and yes, most TV panels included at least one paper on zombies.

For a few years, I attended these conferences regularly, presenting and moderating and kibitzing, and I even went so far as to assume the role of television area chair for one of them. I enjoyed being surrounded by people to whom I didn't have to explain my interests and who didn't laugh patronizingly when I told them I was writing a book about cooking shows. But I also didn't completely fit in there either. I learned that there is a continuum of taking TV seriously, and I was not at the ultra-serious end. The mere inclusion of television in these presentations—for example, "Symbolical and Mythological Concepts in the Realm of Fairytale and Fantasy in Supernatural Movies and TV Series: A Study on Narrative Theory"; "Ethics in Film and TV and Heideggerian Thought in Popular Culture"; "Alfred Hitchcock Presents: Authorship and the Lacanian Sinthome in Hitchcock on Television"—didn't necessarily have me running to get a front-row seat. One sure way to deflavorize a TV show—for me—is to subject it to Lacanian discourse analysis. As in all academic disciplines, then, the scholars end up writing only for each other, and really only for tenure and promotion committees (though few on those committees read the actual texts closely if at all, paying attention only to amount of output, journal prestige, and citation counts, which, unfortunately, in these niche areas are not stellar).

Neither the style nor the content of my writing fits comfortably into academia. But I'd still rather be an oddball there—putting up with the indifference to my subject matter that I don't take personally but rather collectively—than have to compete with people writing TV criticism for a living, thereby what I imagine to be ruining a great pleasure by making it a job. In my twenties I worked as a waitress for four months, until I could no longer tolerate the envy I had for the leisurely customers and their eggs Sardou and Belgian waffles. Also, I'm just not competitive or quick enough on my feet to be a journalist (or a waitress).

When *Watching What We Eat* was published, a *Wall Street Journal* reviewer referred to it as "semi-scholarly." A couple of friends were piqued on my behalf by the phrase, but I embraced it. It was neither criticism nor compliment but simply a spot-on description of me. It's all I know how to do. I can be no less and no more scholarly than I am, try as I might in either direction. I have neither a PhD nor a solid grounding in communications theory (as I think you can tell, and you're welcome). I am something of an oddity at my workplace, where most of the non-library faculty are conducting serious research on social and criminal justice that aims to reduce human suffering and make the world a better place. I respect and admire these dedicated people and consider myself fortunate to be working at the same institution. On those grey days of self-doubt, I feel like a frivolous fraud in their midst, but more often I let their passion inspire mine, which just happens to be different from theirs. And I remind myself that if TV has reduced *my* suffering and made *my* world a better place, it must be true for others, so it's not without planetary value. In fact, at a writing boot camp where a mixed-discipline group of faculty shared their writing projects—things like sex trafficking and silenced communities in Latin America—I told them about mine, this book you're reading now, and they all smiled politely without comment. When we broke for lunch, however, the discussion turned to TV, our lingua franca.

When we moved to our new home in 2009, Gerard and I decided—quite easily, no handwringing—to do so without our

TV. It was a bulky dinosaur by that point, and we had already organically transferred a fair amount of our content viewing to computer screens. As much as a TV watcher as we each were (and are), the transition was as painless as cutting the cord to a landline phone, which on the continuum of 0–10 of the pain scale was a 0. Neither of us is particular about audio or video quality and are quite satisfied watching on a shared thirteen-inch laptop, though we did finally invest in a Bose Bluetooth speaker. I am also perfectly happy watching Netflix, HBOGo, the NBC.com app, and Amazon Prime on my iPhone, which is one of the unfashionable small ones lasting long past its expected obsolescence. Each time I watch a program on my phone, I am incredulous. The thing I dreamed about when I was riding in the backseat of the Cutlass on the New York State Thruway, the *Jetsons*-like mini-TV that I could hold in my hand, is spectacular and real.

I find it strange that a significant number of people cannot accept the fact that I don't own a television. John, a fellow TV person and a communications professor, who, when asked by his eight-year-old daughter upon overhearing one of our nostalgia conversations, "What's *Hee Haw*?" seamlessly responded, "An American television variety show featuring country music and rural humor that aired on CBS for a couple of years at the end of the 1960s." To impart such valuable knowledge on young and spongy brains *almost* made me wish I had offspring of my own. John shakes his head and covers his ears every time I remind him that I don't have a TV. To him, I surmise, it's sacrilege, like a music aficionado not having a turntable or a librarian giving over to ebooks (guilty of that, too). How can I take myself seriously? Others find it "hilarious" that I write about TV but don't have one. These people don't seem to realize that most TV history research is done at media archives or on YouTube and would not be possible on the TV in their living room. And have they been living under a rock for the last decade? You don't need a TV anymore to watch TV. It's a piece of furniture, a delivery system, not the magic box it used to be. I am tired of explaining or defending this. But why do they care? Why am I always afraid my brother-in-law is going to gift us a TV (they don't call them sets anymore, ever notice? Probably because you can't set anything atop them), specifically one that would be so huge and heavy that our eighty-year old walls could not support it? Are they insecure about their own TV ownership? What gives? If I wanted a TV, I'd get one. Even when I am at a hotel or a typical American house with a monstrous TV and every channel known on the planet and beyond (which, granted, I usually cannot figure out how to surf if I can even figure which Apple Roku Alexa Fire Stick remote to use and when and if I push the red button on the wrong one the car will start and the water will be shut off and the owners will lose all their money and saved programs), I find myself watching on-demand self-curated DJ style on my iPad standing up at the kitchen counter.

Having no TV (the furniture) suits me for many reasons. I took piano lessons with Mrs. Usdin all through my school-age years. Her living room—where I spent significant cumulative hours waiting for the previous student to finish—was the soul of a warm, eucalyptus-scented intellectual household. Wooden games, geodes, Red Zinger tea, vintage *Peanuts* books, giant coffee table books about art and nature—the whole room felt ensconced in fabric acquired from international travel (remarkably similar to Jeannie's bottle), nary a TV in sight. Occasionally, I heard audio dribs coming from her teenaged son's room—the telltale sounds of the action-adventure genre—but was virtuous and impervious in my classical music-learning, college-bound bubble. My living room is not quite as lush and aromatic as Mrs. Usdin's, but the TV-less atmosphere makes me feel like I've captured a particle of that essence that I always aspired to. My childhood piano is in the room, too, but it mostly serves as a place to set things.

12

Wise TV

Many TV critics insist that we are in a new golden age (I've lost count), the prestige TV era, fostered in large part by the creative autonomy offered by new production outlets like Netflix, Amazon, and Hulu and the freedom to cater to niche audiences or even just artistic expression or whim, in-between-projects and experimental indulgences. It's hard to argue against this. Indeed, the quality is better than ever before. Were the critic John Leonard still among us, he'd say, "I told you so," since he said in 1991, "It used to be that everybody wanted to write a novel. Then for a long time . . . everybody has wanted to write a screenplay. . . . [W]hen [HDTV] comes you will have the best directors perfectly willing to work in this form. And the writers will always go where there's money. Television could become, I hope, much more of a director and writer's medium than a producer's medium. There's no way of predicting." But predict he did, and quite accurately, except that he thought picture quality would be the tipping point, and while technology was definitely a factor—the digital revolution and all its tentacles—there was also a gradual accretion of taste and cultural changes.

Where actors used to feel relegated to TV when film careers floundered, now TV is making stars, just as it did in the 1950s (Jackie Gleason, Milton Berle, Arthur Godfrey). I return to the Farhad Manjoo article I referenced earlier, where he alludes to the brief shining moment when we watched everything in unison, like standing for the national anthem at a baseball game. Well, the title of that article was "How Netflix Is Deepening Our Cultural Echo Chambers," and the rest of the quote goes like this: "As the broadcast era changed into one of cable and then streaming, TV was transformed from a wasteland into a bubbling sea of creativity. But it has become a sea in which everyone swims in smaller schools." The implication, given the negative connotation of "echo chambers," especially in the wake of the 2016 presidential election, as well as the word "but" after the presumed positive connotation of creativity, is that smaller schools are bad. But these miniature charter schools allow the bubbling creativity. And, not to stir up a nasty debate about education, but research has shown us that smaller classes pump out better-prepared fish.

Now there is so much TV content that I can't watch a fraction. There is enough to warrant competing year-end top ten lists. I listen to podcasts where they talk about a lot of it, so I get a sampling of what's going on. My podcast chat shows are rife with regular, non-industry viewer people talking about the "bottle episode" of *Girls* as if "bottle episode" (I had to Google it—you can do the same) was as common parlance as "season finale." There are now myriad podcasts devoted to single TV shows. Not just current fan clubs but historical. There's *The Carson Podcast*, *The Making of Oprah*, *West Wing Weekly*. There are podcasts about every niche imaginable, so it shouldn't be surprising that TV gets attention in this realm, but it's still a thrill to hear people parse characters and cultural influence to the micro detail. While it drives me to distraction when I hear participants in these conversations struggling to remember Esther Rolle's name, I am gratified that they even know *Good Times* existed. Just a middle-aged aside: When I hear young people—anyone younger than me—say, "That was so long ago!" unless the year they refer to begins with a 19, then zip it. That was not a long time ago, my toddler friend. I think some of these adolescents also have a warped sense of recent history. One example of the one thousand I could bitterly share was expressed by an intelligent young journalist on an intelligent writerly podcast. She referred to the "hand-crafted Internet," which I began to soft-focus daydream about from the clunky but oh-so-thrilling mid-1990s, and she record-scratched my reverie with, "in, like, 2007." Did she mean 1997? Because I make that mistake with the decade bridging the turn of the century all the time. If she didn't, then, baby girl, 2007 was, like, one minute ago. The only thing hand-crafted about the internet was Etsy (which was already two by then), though much to my surprise, we were still using MySpace. Anyway, I stopped listening.

A related complaint: in 2018 *New York* magazine's Vulture section published a "100 Essential TV Comedies," which pushed my buttons hard, so hard that it might have broken me. To be fair, they confessed right up front, "In making a list such as this, there's no way to start at the beginning of TV comedy and cover enough ground, so it only includes shows from the past 30 years." But how on earth can you make a list with that title and not even reference *All in the Family*? And as we have been discussing here, before cable there was not the glut of programming that we are forced to rank and categorize these days. It really would not have been that much more labor to add twenty more shows from the previous thirty years, maybe sacrificing some of the albeit good shows that just began airing relative moments before the list went to press (*The Joel McHale Show, Wyatt Cenac's Problem Areas*) or those also albeit good ones that ran only one or two seasons (*Party Down*) and create a comprehensive list. But already I know it would be hard, because *Sports Night* existed for only two blessed seasons, and excluding it would be a clear misstep. I will discontinue this uncharitable and misguided path down which I'm heading, but I will continue my rant.

I know you were born yesterday (you know who you are), but television wasn't. Is it just me or just the current young adult cohort, or is it ever thus? Has the digital revolution made us so future-focused that we forget to pay homage to the past? I grew up in a household with record albums and a stereo turntable with speakers that put music into the room, and everyone listened to the same thing at the same time (like TV), and those records became the music I first learned to appreciate. But it was not *of* my generation. That may not have been your experience, even if you are also my age. But if you are my age, you didn't grow up in a household with everyone listening to their own separate playlists with earbuds. And not even their own personal cassettes on a Walkman, because even that wasn't born until 1979, which means I didn't get one (non-Sony off-brand) until 1982. Is it just me, or are we in a uniquely ahistorical period brought about by on-demand cultural consumption?

I get unreasonably indignant when people don't contextualize or even consider that maybe everything wasn't invented by their peers six months ago for their enjoyment. I recently read an article in the *New Yorker* about the popularity of podcasts and how one of the most downloaded, the serial *Serial*, was sponsored entirely by one advertiser. I could barely finish the article at that point because I was so distracted by the missed opportunity to comment on the fact that this new-fangled-ish medium of podcasting is basically a return to radio, which, in this instance, is mirroring the advertising protocol of radio and TV shows from the 1920s through the 1950s, like Alcoa for *See It Now*, Revlon's *$64,000 Question* or *Texaco Star Theater* or the first televised cooking show, whose full title was *Elsie Presents James Beard in "I Love to Eat,"* anthropomorphizing the Borden mascot. Instead, a Martian who just alighted upon Earth and read that article would be led to believe that this broadcast and advertising system was something innovative and exciting. I'm not saying it's not, but would you please give some nod to the fact that we've been here before? Also, in the article, I cannot help but continue to grouse, a representative from a company that advertises a lot on podcasts and then developed its own branded podcast was quoted as saying, "We view podcasts less as an advertising channel and more as a content channel to win new customers and engage existing customers." The rep must not be aware that a) he just recited the definition of advertising and b) TV and radio began as—and in most senses of the word still are— advertising vehicles. Just because an ad is half an hour long and has a fetching title does not mean it's not an ad.

The point is, once again, what's old is new again, even if lots of people don't recognize it was ever old. And this is not even getting into the idea that art—the *content*—is largely a reinvention of something already in existence. Here we're just looking at *medium*. Technology. I doubt it foretells my dream of us all getting around on horses and having our pet pigeons ferry our mail, because really everything is cyclical. But a girl can dream. And lest I be judged, I confess that sometimes it is I who forget my/our own history. For instance, a colleague recently told me that she enjoys watching old TV shows–seventies and eighties classics like *Sale of the Century*, *Match Game*,

Columbo, *Highway to Heaven*—and I asked her how and where she finds them. She described a setup that includes antennae and broadcast channels. I was enthralled. TV signals through the air? What kind of space age is this? Oh, wait. "It's a smart TV," she explained. (Wise and old TV, I thought to myself. Or might have whispered.) It seems odd to me that broadcast TV, the only TV I knew for most of my life, is called terrestrial, since all forms of TV still seem *extra* so.

Around the mid-2010s, a lot of reboots, remakes, revivals, and sequels (I leave it up to the professional TV critics to deconstruct the differences) started popping up in sitcom form, and I detected not just my own but a collective eye roll each time the announcement of another one came up—*Fuller House*, *Gilmore Girls: A Year in the Life*, and re-somethings of shows that I watched in their entirety in my adult lifetime, which compressed time in a distressing way. *Roseanne*, *Will & Grace*, and *Murphy Brown* got the old band back together. It's as if TV goes into its closet, finds forgotten clothing, and thinks, "Hey, I still look good in this!" and takes it out for a spin. Some of it is delightfully flattering, but some of it does make your butt look big (to wit, the 2008 remake *90210*, despite the majority of the cast being anorexic). Is this a sign of TV breathing its last breath, paying homage with an inconsistent but portentous *This Is Your Life* retrospective? I suspect it's something much less shmoopy. For the first four or so decades of my TV-watching life, it was easy to forget (or never to understand in the first place) that the force behind my pleasure was a bunch of corporate execs. It's still pretty easy to ignore that They (though a much cleverer They) are behind the quality-TV surge. The reboot/revival era is a rude reminder about the power of the bottom line. They (producers? suits? human, mortgage-carrying writers?) know that we (us, people) are suckers for nostalgia, even for events from two years ago. The ideal opportunity for a reboot, in my snooty opinion, is the case of *Cosmos: A Spacetime Odyssey*, where, in 2014 Neil deGrasse Tyson reprised the role of Carl Sagan in the 1980 *Cosmos: A Personal Voyage*. Not *Mad About You*. The 2017 *One Day at a Time* was, in musical terms, a cover, reviving and paying homage to a bygone creation (in both cases produced by Norman Lear), loosely maintaining the original premise but replacing the original characters with ones that represent an updated demographic and current social and cultural issues. I hear it's good. I'm not not watching to be an obstinate purist. I've just got enough on my TV tray, and if I want to watch *One Day at a Time* or *Murphy Brown*, I'll scrounge on YouTube clips of the original.

What's the equivalent of record albums, aka vinyl, for TV? A BetaMax player and a library of cumbersome, rattling tapes are not exactly hipster accouterments. That's partially because they are hideous and take up a wall of one's home, unlike the sexy slimness of LPs and the sleek modern turntables. But there's also a difference between *Led Zeppelin Remasters* and a reboot of *Battle of the Network Stars*. While both milk the commercial potential of nostalgia, the former is improving the sensory characteristics of something already great without disturbing its original form, whereas the latter is not doing that one bit. But if you think that a TV person (are we not connoisseurs?) is not going to get as pretentiously passionate about the flaws in an *X-Files* revival the way a music aficionado (I want that descriptor, too) would write you off as a cretin for even suggesting that [insert nuanced music thingy], then you need to attend more popular culture conferences.

Somewhere in this second decade of the twenty-first century, the talk of TV in the mediasphere finally matches the voices in my head. The porridge is just the right temperature: serious but not too serious. Neither academic nor Farley-esque gush nor mere synopses nor picks & pans. The media and entertainment outlets have increased and widened so much (the paradoxical conditions necessary for narrowcasting) that there is room for everything, and TV finds at long last a huge and welcoming niche in this hybrid zone—smart (though not always wise and old) talk about TV. At some point, to be honest, however, it became too much of a good thing. If "peak TV" has transpired, then "peak TV criticism" must follow. It seems every hour I find out about another TV critic/person who has an impressive backlog of articles about TV published in an Atlanta-area or Pacific Northwest alternative weekly and who has a Twitter following equal to half the population of the United States—how do *they* all know him/her/them?—that I feel an enormous pressure to read but usually don't get around to. I exist in a constant state of missing out in multiple arenas. I'm sure most of what I've written in this book has been penned previously in different words, and if the authors happen to be reading this, they might be of a mind to accuse me of plagiarism. Or at best complain to me before their 3.2 million Twitter followers, "Try doing a little research, you lazy slag. I wrote about this three years ago." But must I seek out and read every respected critic's take on Phoebe Waller-Bridge's *Fleabag* or *The Marvelous Mrs. Maisel*? I swear, sharp and like-minded TV person, I have not discovered your oeuvre though you have eighty-five Twitter followers I know.

The new platforms for unearthing and consuming content allow for and even anticipate—moreover, encourage—binge watching, a term that didn't exist until 2013 or so. Binge watching is superior, I tell myself as I finish off half a season of *Portlandia* when four hours earlier I said I was too tired to watch an average feature-length movie. No one feels the need to fess up to binge reading, do they? I wonder if people saved up those Dickens serials in 1860 so it felt more binge-y. Don't you feel more connected to a book, more virtuous, when you read seventy-five pages at a stretch than if you read only two pages every night before bed? I like to let shows pool, so I can watch at least two episodes in a row, if not more. The wait is not easy, especially if you enjoy reading about or listening to what people are saying about a show and need to avoid spoilers, but it's worth it. When I am forced to watch a show in "real time" with six commercials every five minutes, I begin to lose focus and start to question my motives and desires, which could be the unraveling of everything. I get that same panicky feeling I did when Ray Bolger's scarecrow started losing chunks of his straw. "Is that all he is?" I wondered, horrified. "Just a bunch of straw through and through? Soon he'll disappear!" It is far from the days of everyone watching the same thing at the same time, which I romanticized earlier as if it held the existential significance of us all looking up at the same moon, but the genie is out of the bottle. I definitely prefer Made for Me TV to Must See TV. (Don't boss me!) And it should come as no surprise. I've moved along the path with TV all along; we've grown up together.

In the second decade of the twenty-first century, journalistic writing about TV has entered—pardon the use of the phrase—a golden age. That's the language I speak. This fact hit me in the face when I was struggling to come up with yet another academic spin on something I actually liked in order to churn out another article for my CV. It was about podcasting and again was something I came about honestly. I was on sabbatical writing my book about Dr. Joyce Brothers, listening to podcasts to entertain me during my snack/procrastination breaks, and I found that they did more than that. I expound on their impact in an essay in the *Chronicle of Higher Education* (because tenure-track faculty members are conditioned to capitalize on every single thought we have; let no persistent thought go unpublished). I worked on the podcasting article little by little, never too excited about the rendering of my initial beloved idea, and struggled to find ways to awkwardly plunk some theory into it. Then about a year into that plodding process, I read a two-thousand-word piece (one-fifth the length of a scholarly journal article, with 100 percent fewer endnotes) in the *New Yorker* by Sarah Larson, who summed up my entire article in a sentence: "Listen to enough episodes and you begin to consider the wild biographies of writers and artists in relation to your own attempts to pursue your dreams." Any regular listener to podcasts knows this to be true, understands that that is why he continues to listen, and requires no evidence other than his own experience. But I still wrote the article in the way that was expected of me, trying to find a handful of scholars who also said what Larson said, but in a less comprehensible way in a lower-circulation publication. If anyone were to ever in a million years ask me what my article was about (perhaps a Western European scholar will stumble across the abstract), I'd send them a freely available link to Larson's.

I know I talk about the *New Yorker* a lot. I bought the idea that I was pummeled with in J-school that it's really the only publication that matters. But I do believe the writing therein is the best around. Emily Nussbaum, the magazine's TV critic since 2011, won the Pulitzer for criticism in 2016 when her conominees included the *New York Times* film critic and the *New Yorker*'s theater critic. The following year the *New Yorker* produced its first TV issue (it had been publishing style, money, and food issues annually for many years). What allowed these marvelous, celebration-worthy turns of events? Answering that would be an academic treatise, and, if I haven't made it clear enough, I am out of that game. But the too-loud dinner-party-banter answer I offer here is: TV matters and finally people are really starting to get that message.

The *New Yorker* also serves to illustrate a sea change in attitudes about television in the twenty-first century. Here I return to Roseanne, who in February 1996 was invited to guest edit an issue devoted to women by embattled star-romancer editor Tina Brown. It was surely a stunt—Brown loved stirring things up—but of all places, the venerable *New Yorker*! To the devout Eustace Tilley absolutists, it was Roseanne sullying the "Star-Spangled Banner" all over again. This is the sort of small upper-middle-class earthquake that provokes some to read civilization its last rites, but others (that include me) to hail it as a sign of progress. Fast-forward two decades to 2016, and we see that very same magazine, now helmed by Brown's revered, Pulitzer Prize–winning, Russia-expert successor, David Remnick, who interviewed Lena Dunham on the *New Yorker Hour* radio show, talking earnestly about the themes and implications of *Girls* and popping a champagne bottle to celebrate her thirtieth birthday on the air. Barr and Dunham, one could argue, occupy similar spaces in popular culture—both are provocateurs, celebrate their non-normative body sizes and perspectives, and create highly successful TV programs that deliver social commentary enveloped in velvety chocolate and crunchy bits. The takeaway is that TV was anointed a high art or a high enough art that it was invited to hang out with the smart, posh kids. The road to quality TV was gradual, and its evolution is chronicled by lots of smart TV critics. You can go read them. I'm just going to rest here and enjoy the moment.

13

Peace, Love, and O. J.

Roseanne Cash has confessed, on public radio air, to an obsession with Toni Tennille. She loved the *Captain & Tennille* variety show and watched it in secret, because it wasn't cool, she said. "It was a guilty pleasure." I know what she means, but I'm going to nitpick anyway. I wouldn't call that a guilty pleasure. Guilt implies something naughty, like the proverbial porno mag shoved under the teenaged boy's mattress. And something you might actually boast about to your mates. I think what Roseanne Cash feels is shame, something hidden that one would be loathe to let *anyone* (other than a public radio audience) know about. I used to feel shame about my secret crush on Danny Bonaduce until I realized people harbored secrets far worse, like crushes on Ted Nugent. Like Roseanne Cash, I sometimes recognized that the things I loved weren't cool at the time, but it never bothered me. I knew being into TV wasn't as clubby or geeky or serious as being into music or movies or theater. My TV dedication marches alongside my predilection for food over alcohol. With apologies to the alcohol-addicted for this crude and potentially triggering overstatement, slamming shots can look sexy on its face, whereas compulsively shoveling food into your face never does.

TV is not and never was a *guilty* pleasure for me. But that doesn't mean I haven't had moments of ambivalence. Despite having lived for more than five decades, representing a lot of time and experience with which to hone and assert my thoughts about television, I think I lie to myself at times. In more recent years, I would joke about how watching TV is research, and it has been true in cases, but it is fundamentally a pleasurable (if occasionally educational or informative) activity. Maybe it's aging or maybe it's the current cult of "self care," but I have relatively only lately recognized the physical and psychological value of pleasure and appreciate that TV has provided that for me all these years.

In his 2018 article on *The Good Place*, *New York Times* culture writer Sam Anderson described how the show's creator, Mike Schur, and perhaps the culture at large, is thirsty in these seeming end-times for morality tales like those that used to be baked into the plots of early sitcoms and then dropped into "very special episodes," like when Edith was raped, Maude got pregnant at age forty-seven, and Roseanne's sister, Jackie, was abused by her boyfriend. But as much as the morality craving makes for a relevant narrative, it's not a new trope.

My journalism professor Jay Rosen, a prolific media critic whose thinking and writing I have long admired, the one with whom I argued in favor of *Roseanne* as more than empty entertainment, denounced the dearth of sincerity in the culture. It was 1996. Think Jerry Seinfeld and Chandler Bing. A time when mainstream pop culture was, as retroactively described by journalist Jen Chaney, "steeped in postmodernism: irony, satire, and sarcasm." I am still feigning to grasp an operational definition of "postmodern," but irony, satire, and sarcasm were most definitely the Petri dish cells that gave rise to our *90210* newsletter spawned during that era. They are also braided into my DNA. So when Professor Rosen rhetorically asked the class, in his earnest and persuasive manner, "What's so funny about peace love and understanding?" his sly invocation of Nick Lowe/Elvis Costello weakened my knees and resolve for a barely detectable millisecond. My answer then and now, controversial and hyperbolic: "Everything is funny." I know all comedians would agree with me, so it's not like I'm taking some unique and bold stance. But at the time I felt shaky about it, since I was figuring out what I believed as I was saying it. I'm still figuring out what I believe as I write this. Sometimes I feel a little guilty (not shameful) that sarcasm and irony are my crutches—really it's that I cannot abide excessive or pedantic earnestness—but again, there are worse vices.

A lot of us watch *Seinfeld* reruns and long for the deliberate lack of hugging and learning. Maybe people (e.g., me) watch *The Good Place* and *Modern Family* for the high laugh-per-minute ratio and Easter eggs, *despite* the sappy undertones and happy endings. You can't just go around making generalizations about the national mood and desires or the signaling of a mass desire for morality lessons—well, you can, I know I love to generalize, but not without some annoying person (e.g., me) reminding us that people are different. Some people don't like to watch characters they don't like, for example, which is something I could never relate to. I love watching characters I hate. Given the popularity of TV antiheroes, I can see I'm not alone.

Most of my full-throated defense of television relates to content and form and giving it its rightful place in the realm of the arts. But behavior is another matter, and naturally, this goes back to childhood. Most of us in my peer group came up happily watching TV but also knowing that it was a treat and therefore something that could be consumed beyond moderation and something whose source could be cut off, devastatingly, at any moment. Some parents put limits on their kids' watching to *x* number of hours per week or in exchange for some deed like completing homework or washing the dishes or another unsavory deal. I remember the first time I met a peer who said her parents didn't allow her and her siblings to watch TV. I was horrified. How could she get along in life not knowing the theme song to *Gilligan's Island*? What did she do if she didn't watch TV? Churn butter? Darn socks? Read and converse and play board games and become skilled in sports and outdoor activities? Without sharing the same cultural references, I doubted that she and I could ever be true friends. At the same time, I knew there was something that was considered superior about her family's lifestyle, and I carried the knowledge like a small chip, placed near but not quite on my shoulder. Nowadays, when I hear someone proudly or dismissively claim they don't watch TV, I may envy their whittling skills, but I also feel sorry for them.

Phrases like "glued to the set" and research on the worrisome brain-rotting effects of excessive screen time have given TV a bad reputation. The word "addiction" is often tossed around in its presence. David Foster Wallace wrote that watching TV "may become malignantly addictive only once a certain threshold of quantity is habitually passed, but then the same is true of Wild Turkey." I enjoy alcohol and got better at defining moderation as I got older. I can say the same about my TV consumption, even though it might not always look like it from an outsider's p.o.v. I agree with Wallace to an extent, but I also think intentionality must be taken into account, which is not a modification afforded to problem drinkers. Emily Nussbaum must watch a ghastly amount of TV, but we wouldn't call her an addict. Or perhaps she has just found the ideal enabling profession.

While I stand by my youthful pro-sarcasm crusade, I have to reckon with its vagaries and nuances now that I have nearly doubled in years and quintupled in experience (the algorithm of age). Revisiting the ideas of Rosen and Postman and Miller and Wallace (not that they all agree on everything, but I often disagree with them), I have to admit to getting their drift. That's very humbling (and cliché) to admit, but I'm trying to be a big person here. I don't know if I would have come around to this sage and mature point of view were it not for the internet, but given the nature of things, surely some other type of media would have caused me an equal amount of self-deflation eventually. Largely because I am able to see them taking place with internet behavior, both my own and that of every single human around me, I cannot deny the ill effects of inordinate media consumption.

Social media is now the time suck that TV used to be and still is for a lot of people. While I try to justify looking at Twitter as my window to the world, my temperature gauge, yadda yadda, that excuse is a bunch of bullshirt. I feel sick and self-hating when I cannot stop scrolling through Twitter. I don't remember ever feeling that way about TV. Because I don't have a television, I don't even have the setup to watch any old thing, whatever's on. I watch deliberately and pointedly, as well as compulsively and obsessively, but never mindlessly. I'm not sure I was ever a mindless watcher. When I do have access to and free rein with a TV and try to give it a whirl, if I can't find something to sink into, if I press through all the channels available and don't excitedly land on something (sometimes, an unexpected and delightful something will suck me in just when I really need it, like when I was housesitting the same 2016 week that George Michael, Carrie Fisher, and Debbie Reynolds died, and I comforted myself with lots of George Michael videos as well as a random Michael Jackson documentary), I will give up and try to read. No FOMO, I saw what there was, and among those 236 channels, there was nothing for me. I should only press through once, but often I go backward, to make sure I really gave it a shot. After two turns, I feel pretty disgusted with myself and with modern society.

Watching TV (as opposed to channel pressing) for a prolonged period does not result in lost-time regret or post-watching shame for me. It's like oversleeping. You know you probably should have gotten up earlier, but somehow your body needed that. Right? "Joe Briefcase might have been happy enough when watching," writes David Foster Wallace, "but it was hard to think he could be too terribly happy about watching so much." Terribly happy? No. I'm not doing a jig or anything, but I don't feel like I've wasted time after bingeing a series, for example. I've done "research," learned something, prepared myself to take part in the cultural conversation, been stimulated by the cleverness, beauty, humor, and creativity, or bathed in pleasure neurochemicals.

As much as I enjoy not taking things too seriously, I'm no sociopath. I am capable of hugging and learning. And I won't deny some of the dark times TV and I have endured.

Many parallels have been drawn between the outcome of the *People of the State of California v. Orenthal James Simpson* case in 1995 and that of the 2016 US presidential election, largely vis-à-vis the reaction to the verdicts in both cases. Indeed, the two events immediately crashed against one another in my own experience. Given that 2015 was the twentieth anniversary of the Simpson decision, O. J. was already very much on the minds of lots of Americans. Two excellent series aired in 2016 about the crime and the trial that helped revive that period. Ezra

Edelman's *O.J.: Made in America* was a five-part documentary, scrupulously researched and as riveting as the days of the actual trial. I purchased a temporary pass for a sketchy-sounding TV service to watch it, because it was broadcast on ESPN, which was on regular TV and which was and is a device that I did not and do not possess. The other was a critically acclaimed, ten-episode dramatized iteration, *American Crime Story: The People v. O. J. Simpson*, starring Cuba Gooding Jr. as O. J. but, significantly for me, costarred John Travolta (Robert Shapiro), Rob Morrow (Barry Scheck), Malcolm Jamal Warner (Al Cowlings), and David Schwimmer (Robert Kardashian).

These four actors were pinned to other TV eras. Warner tugged at me because he was Theo all grown up, because he was just trying to be a good friend to the Juice, and because his (and America's) longtime TV dad had recently been disgraced due to serial rape charges. Morrow was relegated in my mind to Dr. Joel Fleischman in *Northern Exposure*, and Schwimmer was originally cast in my archives from his mere four-episode appearance in *The Wonder Years*. *Northern Exposure* and *The Wonder Years* were part of the early 1990s fare but somehow felt entirely apart from *90210* and *Thirtysomething*. They were too subtle and smart to lovingly mock in a social group or underground zine. Maybe these were my Goldilocks sweet spots. When *Friends* exploded on Must See TV Thursday only two years later, in 1994, it was as if Schwimmer had been a crush from elementary school, someone I no longer recognized and could not reconcile as the same person, so distant was Ross from his shaggy-haired (much more attractive physiognomically, I felt) boyfriend of Olivia d'Abo in an ersatz 1970-ish context.

But John Travolta. We had a real history. Vinnie Barbarino stole my heart in 1975. I tried to quit him, but while *Welcome Back, Kotter* was still on the air, he triple-whammied me with the release of *Saturday Night Fever* in 1977 and *Grease* in 1978. Other than a class clown who made me blush whenever he accidentally looked my way in fifth grade, and the fleeting frisson with Felix in the twelfth, I had never and would never again have a thing for a sweet, dopey boy, and Travolta's appeal to me remains inexplicable (though not as baffling as my thing for the adult, drug-addicted Danny Bonaduce). There was a decade-plus stretch, after Travolta's overexposure, where he was out of the spotlight and flattened into the popular mind-set as a cheesy has-been. Martin Amis wrote a gratifying profile of Travolta for the *New Yorker* in 1995 but never once mentioned Barbarino. He even used phrases describing Travolta such as "baffled sweetness of the young Travolta's smile" and "obtuse and something of a point-misser." Maybe Amis assumed, wrongly, that *New Yorker* readers don't watch sitcoms, or maybe he was unaware, tragically, of *Welcome Back, Kotter*. I had joined in on the career downfall dismissal, of course, to protect my own pride and push down my tender feelings, but then *Pulp Fiction* happened. Because I arrived late to the theater, I had to sit in the front row and tilt my head back to see the whole screen. That may be part of why that movie had such a lasting impact on me (in a good way, courtesy of my immunity to dramatized graphic human slaughter). I immediately began proudly renewing my vows to Travolta, and we've been together ever since, our religious (or lack thereof) differences notwithstanding. Whenever he appears on a screen, my heart gets a little tickly, and I find whatever he is doing a little adorable and funny, even as (or maybe especially as) an overly eye-browed portrayal as a real-life litigator.

It was not until I finished watching *The People vs. O. J.*, which I didn't succumb to until at least a year after everyone was talking about it, that I took stock of how that event pulled a lot of my TV experience into a nexus. The actual coverage of the crime and the trial dominated TV for months in 1994 and 1995, bridging the time that I left Boston for New York. I distinctly recall overhearing an exchange between two men outside my local Dunkin' Donuts in 1995, after some brief break in the wall-to-wall trial coverage, that went like this. "How ya doin'?" one said, and the other replied, "Okay. Everything's back to normal now. O. J.'s back on TV." It was one of those early, heady moments of meta-awareness about TV that I filed away in my mental TV Matters folder, feeling at once smart and sassy as I was heading off to New York to become a member of the cultural illuminati but also genuinely curious and moved (if not somewhat disturbed) by that comment.

As if all these touchstones convening for my sentimental and intellectual benefit were not enough, one of the episodes of *The People vs. O. J.* was called "Marcia, Marcia, Marcia." Seeing this title had the same effect on me as the *Kimmy Schmidt* episode where Carole Kane cried like the fake Native American. "Marcia, Marcia, Marcia" was an oft-bandied reference to the *Brady Brunch* episode where the put-upon middle sister has had it to up to her blonde ringlets with the praise lavished upon her golden older sister. While the reference was in name only (the put-upon prosecutor, Marcia Clark, was in fact far more Jan-like and would have been more aptly represented by the episode title, "Johnnie, Johnnie, Johnnie," but the association would be much too obscure), it gave me disproportionate pleasure. I decided there and then that the O. J. Simpson murder trial and its twenty-year aftermath perfectly encapsulated my relationship with television. And not just my relationship, but America's. Would any of us have the name Kardashian in our household lexicon, you really have to wonder, and would there be children in the world named Saint, North, and Chicago

West if not for the O. J. Simpson trial? (Simpson was arrested for robbery and kidnapping just a month before the premiere of *Keeping up with the Kardashians* in 2007—too soon to add that to the list of charges against him.)

Back to the actual trial, in 1995, specifically the verdict in October of that year, which lives in the category of "where were you when . . . ?" moments. Unlike the shared trauma of seeing the Challenger explosion or mass vicarious embarrassment of Janet Jackson's nipple exposure during Super Bowl XXVIII halftime, where you were—especially if you were watching in a group and especially if that group was of mixed race—when you heard the Simpson verdict had the power to tell you far more about yourself and your cultural biases and assumptions than you ever wanted to know. I don't think I need to elaborate much more other than to confess that I learned in the span of ten seconds that I had been living under a rock until age thirty and that outrage and shame can exist simultaneously in the same dyspeptic gut. When I contrast that moment with watching the 2009 Obama inauguration projected on a giant screen along with a large group of mixed-race (and likely fairly mixed political leanings) colleagues, I could not control my tears of joy. There is definitely a direct through line connecting the strong, if confused and complex, emotions in those two high-intensity situations, but I am unable or unwilling to articulate it.

Flip to November 8, 2016. The through line continues. Apparently, I had never moved out from under that rock, but rather to another similar plot crowded with so many neighbors that I didn't notice the blocked view—like some kind of horror movie Levittown. In a *Saturday Night Live* skit aired just after the election, it seemed as though there had been a hidden camera inside the enormous TV in my neighbor's living room where a group of us watched the returns ooze in. (As Edward R. Murrow was to WWII, Walter Cronkite to Vietnam, and Peter Arnett to the Gulf War, so CNN's Jake Tapper was to the 2016 election. The look of consternation fixed on his face early on, and it transferred like a regrettable tattoo onto all of ours.) The only differences between the skit and our actual situation was that everyone in front of our TV had a phone on which they were also monitoring the news, and we did not have commentary from Dave Chappelle and Chris Rock or any other people of color. Though we would have ignored their prognoses just like the white people in the skit did. At the start of the evening on which we would welcome the nation's first woman president (I told myself, still superstitiously wearing my solidarity pantsuit), I thought, "Aw! Look at TV still uniting us around the hearth. All is not lost in this atomistic modern age." Toward the end of the evening, though most of us were still sitting there together, and Gerard was right beside me, I was alone in that room. We all were. No one spoke and we received no comfort from our togetherness. I thanked my neighbor for the snacks and walked across the hall, numb. We are not united around the hearth or seemingly anywhere else. Not by a long shot.

TV brought such bad news. Lots of people said TV was a culprit, in this election outcome. True enough, TV had made this president in unprecedented ways (though social media allegedly got him elected). Earlier I said I didn't begrudge the messenger when it brought me bad news. I didn't this time either. I didn't even feel like throwing anything at it. Don't get me wrong. I recognize the hell that TV hath wrought. It caters to the lowest common denominator, tries to please everybody, cares only about the bottom line, mindlessly replicates mindless successful formats, sensationalizes news, obscures facts, and is currently missing an opportunity, as the global temperature rises to unprecedented heights, to tell everyone that the sky is actually falling (seems like an appropriate use of the Emergency Broadcast System). But who or what is "it"? The furniture isn't doing that, nor are the broadcast or cable systems. Human beans are making all the crap and bad decisions. But, let's face it, the box and the dissemination systems exacerbate the problem. (Are you now thinking about the NRA slogan about who or what kills people? Sorry.) But here's another medium-is-the-message take on it: If you tend to blame TV for the sometimes evil things it does, consider it like a wild animal. You might be distraught when you see a lion devour an antelope (on a nature documentary or in person), but the lion isn't evil. It's just doing what it was born to do and what it needs to do to survive. A wild animal cannot be tamed. A lion is too big to fail.

James Carville's famous campaign phrase "the economy, stupid" comes in handy so often because it distills ideas down to their nuclei—what really matters? What are we talking about here? With TV, it's the image, stupid. It's what separates it from radio. And it is powerful and can play tricks on you. The legendary story of the 1960 television debate between Kennedy and Nixon is still probably the best example of the bonus information delivered by an image; those who *heard* it broadcast on the radio thought Nixon had won handily, and those who *saw* the sweaty bastard seated with Mr. Cool thought the opposite. My parents' generation had Kennedy's funeral and horrific images from Vietnam, the "living room war," to fasten their memories. Every generation has its devastatingly memorable or memorably devastating example.

On the morning of September 11, 2001, listening to NPR on my shower radio in my uptown Manhattan apartment, I heard the first report of a plane apparently hitting one of the World Trade Center towers. In my imagination, a little prop jet had—whoopsie!—strayed out of bounds and clipped its wing on the edge of the roof or a radio tower gizmo. That was the image I took from the local NPR host's neutral tone and scant information. I started getting ready for work, and about fifteen minutes later when I mentioned that little byte to my boyfriend, just in the way of making conversation, his eyes flew wide open and he rushed to turn on the TV. The improbable little cartoon I had previously arranged in my head vanished. On the screen, we saw [description redacted]. I was frozen in place and all my surroundings seemed to lose color. I could not take my eyes off the screen for what felt like seventy-two hours.

If you gave me the opportunity to rewatch the scenes I saw that morning, I would ask you how much I could pay you to make sure I never saw them again. Any unbidden images I do come across from that event still hit me with nearly the same force. I realize that my interpretation from the radio was completely illogical, but this is the billionth example of how a picture—especially those on TV—paints a thousand words. If I wanted to make a particular argument, I could use this example and the sweaty Nixon one to try to convince you that images tell the truth because they expose everything. But you've been around the block enough to know how images can be misused and manipulated. And you've seen enough nature documentaries to know how a poisonous spider can camouflage itself.

TV can't subsist on selling Super Elastic Bubble Plastic and the Neighborhood of Make-Believe. The highs and the lows make it the complex creature that it is, and the reality of its potential power further upholds my thesis.

14

I Rest My Case

When I was in my twenties and searching under all the couch cushions for a direction in life, I was a sucker for that touchy-feely self-help genre of career books, the kind that I found in any number of ambergris-scented, wind-chime-tinkling, crystal-purveying bookstores in and around Cambridge, Massachusetts. I repeatedly assessed the color of my parachute and wanted to believe the principle of *Do What You Love, the Money Will Follow*. If I were on a podcast where the host was asking me—the voice of my generation or at least *a* voice of only children born in western New York state in 1965 who religiously watched the original *Mickey Mouse Club* in syndication—what I would tell my younger self, it would be a slightly tweaked version of that: Do what you love and there will likely be no money in it, but find a day job you can tolerate by the time you're forty-two and you really can have it all. If you don't find inspiration in my journey, then I don't know how to help you. I know mine is not the story of a punk rock star who was bullied as a kid for liking "weird" music and clothes. But proudly and loyally loving something that's derided by fancy, smart people, or that you shouldn't love too much or in the wrong way, may not make you a millionaire, but provided it's not hurting anyone or anything, it can give you joy. So stick with it, kid. Don't let them bring you down, etc. Not long ago, I saw a young man mention his thesis on Twitter in order to get the attention of its subject, Kim Kardashian. It did, but that's not my point. One of the commenters asked, "How did you get to write a paper like that?" You just do it. And if your professor says your topic is unacceptable because it's not serious or doesn't matter, I strongly encourage you take a stand, backed up with easily found research, or transfer to a different section.

In 2007 a scholar from Australia named Alan McKee wrote a short but affecting essay called "Why Do I Love Television So Very Much?" for the TV studies journal *FLOW* (the same one that accepted my TV cooking show parody article). As of this writing, more than a decade later, it still shows up on the site's main page as the most popular post as measured by the volume of comments it provoked. Many people have written about the value and virtues of TV. While Bob Thompson is my greatest American hero, there have been many other scholars around the world who have done so, and now the elevated status of TV criticism itself signals a mantle of respect that defenders of the lively art have sought for so long. John Hartley, another scholar working out of Australia (no coincidence there; Australians are passionate intellectual champions of TV, and one day I'll get around to learning why that is).

McKee pits the historically-thought-of low-culture TV against high-culture Art. The notion of the latter makes him angry for its exclusivity and buzz-killing superiority complex. TV, on the other hand, welcomes everyone, even the art snobs who, if they deign to or accidentally watch *The Simpsons*, for instance, are treated with inside jokes just for them. It's hard not to quote every other sentence of this delightfully petulant treatise, so I urge you to go to flowjournal.org and read it. I'll just share this one for now: "Watching television makes me a better person. It reinforces my best qualities. When I'm watching television I'm genuinely interested in the lives it shows me and the ways that are different from mine. I am joyful in the encounters it offers with difference." I have heard plenty of people say these exact words about the experience of reading novels, spouting the now scientifically supported and much flaunted fact that it encourages the development of empathy. But I can also hear many arguing that we typically don't encounter difference when watching TV, because we naturally lean toward watching shows that demographically reflect us. That is probably true (I have a gut feeling that this may be less true of novels for reasons I will leave someone else to investigate). And there are all kinds of criticisms of TV shows' representations of minor and minority characters as being too flat, and I am sure that's true, too—the "weighty expectations of universality," as Joy Press puts it (when talking about *Girls*) in her book *Stealing the Show: How Women Are Transforming Television*. But if we don't ask a still life hanging in the Metropolitan Museum of Art to be all things to all people and to repair a host of social ills, why would we demand that of *Friends* or *The Fresh Prince of Bel-Air* or *Fresh off the Boat*?

McKee offers numerous reasons to laud TV while indirectly jabbing at high-culture snobs. Like this, from his edited volume tantalizingly titled *Beautiful Things in Popular Culture*: "Just as marginalized ethnic groups in society are statistically more likely to be bilingual than members of dominant ethnic groups—because they know a native language and that of the dominant group in society—so users of popular aesthetic systems are likely to be aesthetically bilingual." I know he's not referring to Spanish, ASL, and Ubbi Dubbi, but in describing the plight of the lively-arts champions as being aware of the "other" arts in addition to their own bailiwick, they need to be able to speak high- and low-culture patois. This squares with my own long-held belief that people who are aware of and appreciative of the popular arts are generally better rounded than those who reflexively scoff at anything that is outside the canon.

Not that the world of TV is free of snobbery. Every subculture has its own hierarchy—music (see *High Fidelity*), computer programming (see *Silicon Valley*), food (see *Ratatouille*). Twenty-first-century TV people natter on about single-camera this and jump-cut that. And there's the prestige vs. non-prestige (what should we call it? TV?). I am a consummate snob, based on the fact that I strongly dislike reality TV (and reference the *New Yorker* incessantly), something I've done a poor job of concealing in this book. But I've forced myself to watch some of it, so I can hate it with confidence. If you're going to broadcast the fact that you hate something, or even if you're going to quietly allow yourself to believe that you hate something merely on principle or hearsay or virtue signaling, you should at least run toward the problem at least once, so you know that you really hate it and maybe why.

As culture critic Lili Loofbourow has written, "You can jump ship, of course: forget the we altogether, relax, and enjoy your own perceptions. But if you do that, you'll never be taken seriously as a thinker, scholar, creator, or critic. For many people, that's been a small price to pay." The "we" she refers to is the powerfully influential groupthink that inevitably affects broad cultural judgments and suppresses the individual ones. Even though Loofbourow is writing about woman-produced art, many of her examples are television products, and so she aligns with McKee and his high-art screed—and "television" could be substituted for "female" (I like that I just had a reason to write that strange, dangerously misinterpretable phrase)—when she lambastes the "smug inattention" toward non-male art for centuries and worries about "a culture defined by casually diagnostic (and artistically cataclysmic) dismissals." Basically, dismissing stuff out of hand is lame. Remember my dear Jenny Diski saying essentially the same thing about the question of eating animals? "It's not possible (or attractive) to be better than we are simply by morally withdrawing from the mess." And while I'm on a spate of callbacks, remember Dan Engber way back at the beginning talking about the "we-ness" of TV watching, the way the "first-person plurality of taste within your social group" cuts off the possibility of conversation? If I wanted to keep this daisy chain going, I could invoke Postman and his beef about electronic entertainment putting a big wrench into vital public discourse. So that continuum I just unintentionally illustrated, starting with Alan McKee and ending with Neil Postman, could be interpreted as us all arguing for the same thing, which is: let's talk about everything all the time. Consider it done.

I reread McKee's essay during a break of my *Crazy Ex-Girlfriend* binge (three seasons of eighteen forty-two-minute episodes called for a full-on boot camp of viewing and also called for Gerard threatening to call me *his* crazy ex-girlfriend). Even after all my preaching about the value of television, I still hungrily consume and reconsume others' well-argued claims in that direction. And even in middle age, after fifty years of watching and loving television, and despite all my swaggering assertions in what you've read here, I still grab at opportunities to justify the value of the pleasure it gives me. That may have more to do with my desire for attention than with combating perceived societal shaming, but I can count even among my acquaintances a few who cannot suppress a judgmental smirk or hide their "smug inattention" from behind the pages of *Middlemarch*, which they are rereading for the fourth time, and from which they claim to derive the same pleasure that I do from rewatching *The Office* (the British one).

Since the turn of this century, almost any essay you read about TV brings up the maxim about how we're a fractured culture thanks to the internet plus the zillion cable channels piled on by personal devices. Though true, stating it in every intro is boring. In his article on *The Good Place*, Sam Anderson put a more visceral and melancholic twist on that same idea without using the words "fractured," "splintered," or "atomized": "Sitcoms no longer sit anywhere near the vital center of American culture. We are not a nation of families squeezing onto couches to watch can't-miss programming. Our entertainment metabolisms have sped up and scattered in a thousand directions." As much as TV was and is maligned by so many doomsayers who claim our mindless behavior is signaling the breakdown of meaningful interpersonal communication, in the typical sociocultural cycles of fear-change-fear, many of us seem to be pining for the days of regular old TV watching in the den.

The concept of TV as electronic hearth has been knocking about for decades, used alternately to boost or excoriate, depending on who's selling what or trying to make which optimistic or dark argument. The central place of TV in the space of the modern middle-class home has been chronicled on dozens of TV shows themselves. The last scene of the opening sequence of *The Simpsons* captures this idea to a tee: one by one, each family member is pulled from scattered directions, landing on the couch in front of the TV, the last image that of the TV screen showing credits of the show we're on our own couches watching. Another example: Just about every moment of every episode of the British sitcom *The Royle Family* (its original seasons straddled the millennium) took place in the front room in the glow of the telly. It might sound parodic and/or pathetic, but Royles fans were witnesses to the poignancy of that family's communion—every single night—over the course of a decade. We viewers love these families that seem dysfunctional on the outside but are gooey and paradoxically aspirational on the inside. And if we're honest, we're looking at our own reflections. "They eat candy bars for dessert every single night!" I said to Gerard, poking fun at the Royles' nonbourgeois eating habits. "We eat candy bars every night," he replied, calling me on my unwokeness with Christopher Hitchens–like alacrity. "A couple rows of a single-origin 80 percent cocoa bar is not the same as a Wagon Wheel/KitKat/Club Biscuit," I subtly pantomimed, just short of actually saying aloud.

A movie scene comes to my mind, too. It was, for me, the most memorable in the quiet and affecting *Nebraska*, the one starring Will Forte and Bruce Dern, where eight men sit almost in rows facing the TV, watching a Bears vs. Lions game, uttering only the dullest of rote conversational contributions about formerly owned vehicles and how long it took to drive somewhere, their faces barely turning from the screen. If this image doesn't remind you of your own family or that of your in-laws, then I'm guessing you were either home schooled or are Amish. These scenes are meant to satirize excessive or mindless TV consumption (or something about men or rural life). The conventional criticism, as Barbara Royle complains while clearing the ashtrays from the coffee table in front of the telly, is "Nobody talks because they're always watching TV!" But we've come far enough from actual TV watching, the way the Royles did it, that it has become a point of nostalgia, as Sam Anderson perhaps unwittingly sets up in his tableau. What loss are we lamenting here? Shouldn't we bid good riddance to our conversation-killing, couch-potato ways?

It turns out that the metaphorical couch *is* what we miss in many cases, and it's a tangible loss. A colleague—not incidentally an anthropologist—told me that she has established an enforced TV-watching period for her family, which includes her husband and two teenaged children. As a corrective to the antisocial bingeing and phone watching, she feels strongly it's the way TV should be watched. She denounces the neoliberal, on-demand, personal choice, niche culture and pines for the quaintness and wholesomeness of watching something together and consuming a complete narrative. It's hard to get them all to agree on what to watch, but she believes it's "the right thing to do." So her children, in a perfect twenty-first-century tech innovation backlash parable, can now feel guilty when they *don't* watch TV.

Sitting around watching TV is a way of communing and not communing at the same time. I would argue that *The Royle Family*, the guys watching the game in *Nebraska*, and me and Gerard, are communing more than a couple looking at their phones, even if they are physically intertwined on a bearskin rug whilst doing so. We and the Royles are more in the same space physically and emotionally. In the UK reality TV show *Gogglebox*, the camera is trained on groups of people in their homes watching and commenting on what they're seeing on TV. Unlike *Mystery Science Theater*, the viewer of *Gogglebox* is not also watching the program. We're looking at their faces, not the backs of their heads. Upon hearing a description of this program, a regular person might sneer and wonder how on earth that could be entertaining. When I—an irregular person—heard about it, I sought it out immediately (despite its Reality categorization), and indeed saw the appeal. Watching the watchers is watching people who are unified, communing, having a laugh or being horrified or disgusted together. I suppose this could all take place if they were watching YouTube as well, but somehow this show feels like a love letter to actual television, the appliance. It might sound like I'm trying desperately to get you to buy into the spiritually beneficial aspects of TV watching, but I really am not. I am, as they say, just saying.

When French writer Antoine de Saint-Exupéry penned his now-famous quote "Love does not consist of gazing at each other, but in looking outward together in the same direction," the shared "high effort" to which he referred was not television, but it fits my purposes like a silken glove. British comedian Jimmy Carr essentially paraphrased him when he said that "happy couples spend forty years laughing at the same things together." This notion applies to my husband and me for just about everything we do in the world, whether we're looking at trees and birds, Showtime performers on the subway, or that nonbiodegradable, single-use dental flosser someone tossed on the sidewalk. And we have a very strong bond when it comes to our screen entertainment. We have our differences—he watched *Lost* and *Battlestar Galactica*, *Black Mirror*, and *Sherlock*. I watch *Lady Dynamite*, *Broad City*, and *High Maintenance*. But we are partners in much more—*Girls*, *The Crown*, *Big Little Lies*, *Animal Airport*, *The Office* (both). And we have anointed ourselves honorary masters of comedy, watching every standup special and YouTube clips of early career-defining late-night talk show appearances. In my prolonged imaginary arguments with my favorite high-culture elitists carping about how TV separates us and inhibits meaningful discourse, I always passionately defend the opposite point.

Also, there's the talking about it (I prefer debriefing *afterward*, unlike the Goggleboxers who talk all through the damn show) that is additional communion aided by time and thought. I suspect that Neil Postman and Dan Engber (he of the solipsistic bubble "we-ness" theory) would sadly shake their heads at the premise of *Gogglebox* or *The Royle Family*. But if we forced them to watch a few episodes of each and hooked them up to a lie detector, I don't believe that either of them would be able to honestly deny the humanity contained in those situations.

I've been on the defensive for so long with regard to TV that a dukes-up position is my resting state. Perhaps I protest too much, even when no one is asking me to, like right now. But I don't need to justify or be defensive any more, at least not with most people, least of all with you. This is probably true for a mix of reasons that include the something-th golden age of TV but also the diversity of the programming and the number of outlets and platforms. Everyone's got a different way to float his or her boat, and it makes little sense to argue or disdain those ways or boats.

If you Google "psychological effects of television" (without quotes; listen to me, I am a librarian), you immediately see lots of negative associations, which are not what comes up if you swap in "music" or "art" or "reading" for television. There's research on the pro-social effects of quality, thoughtful programming on children's learning and development, but there is not much on the intangible benefits for grown-ups. In my book about Dr. Joyce Brothers, I wrote about how her program and others like it made people feel less alone. There's distraction, learning, laughter, etc. But if we treat TV as an art, as we should, then look at all the research there is about how looking at paintings and listening to music or reading a book has healing power.

Programs like *Crazy Ex-Girlfriend*, *Lady Dynamite*, *Flaked*, *Nurse Jackie*, *Enlightened*, and a host of others all feature white, college-educated protagonists like me, but they also feature mental illness or addiction, which are issues that touch many people's lives. Go ahead, imaginary critic sitting next to me on my couch that I did not invite over, just try and tell me that I am wasting my time watching these shows. I will retort that they boldly address formerly taboo subjects, especially daring for sitcoms, and they are entertaining, well-written, destigmatizing, and empathy boosting. And the pleasure that I experience while watching them floods my bloodstream with serotonin, which makes me happier and therefore likely kinder and potentially adding more goodness to the world. I realize that pleasure could likewise be achieved by having a nonreciprocal foot rub or eating something with dulce de leche in or on it. So I'll add that, unlike those activities, television expands my horizons. *Crazy Ex-Girlfriend* made me more open to musical theater (you thought I was going to say more empathetic toward high-functioning mentally ill people, but I'm already quite good at that), *Downton Abbey* and *The Crown* filled in the gaping holes in my British history and government knowledge, and *Breaking Bad* made me wiser to the mechanisms of the opioid scourge. There's something serious lurking in just about every entertainment closet nowadays. This ain't your father's *Father Knows Best*. Betty, Bud, and Kitten sure as heck dealt with earnest issues, but their angst was aspirational, not symptomatic of suicidal ideation. What we have now is "sophisticated" TV. Even reality TV, as fake as it is, can claim to instruct about social class. Not surprisingly, there's a body of scholarship that focuses on the neoliberal dynamic of reality TV, but I will stop myself from telling you about any of that.

Taking stock of my coevolution with TV, I am proud of our survival and achievements over the last half-century. We have gained valuable life experience and confidence and creativity. We hit some bumps, but we made the best of even the 1980s, and we're stronger for it. Together we witnessed the evolution from suntan lotion to sunscreen. We're quite pleased with ourselves at this point. And we're comfortable enough in our own skins that we will even embrace our imperfections, acknowledge rather than hide our most embarrassing traits, and even celebrate some of the most annoying parts of ourselves, perhaps to the dismay of those looking at us, but fork it. Growing old is a privilege.

About the Author

Photography by Arpi Pap

Kathleen Collins writes about television, media, and popular culture, both historical and current. She is the author of *Watching What We Eat: The Evolution of Television Cooking Shows* (Bloomsbury/Continuum, 2009) and *Dr. Joyce Brothers: The Founding Mother of TV Psychology* (Rowman & Littlefield, 2016). Her work has also appeared in the *Journal of Popular Film & Television*, *Critical Studies in Television*, *Journalism & Mass Communication Quarterly*, and *Camera Obscura: Feminism, Culture, and Media Studies*. Her collection of graduate degrees includes counseling psychology, journalism, and library science, and she is a professor and librarian at John Jay College of Criminal Justice in New York City.